More Aster(ix) Anthologies

(Un)bound
Winter 2018/2019

Edges
Fall 2018

Dirty Laundry
Fall 2017

Kitchen Table Translation
Summer 2017

Best of Kweli
Spring 2017

What We Love
Fall 2016

Atravesando
Spring 2016

available for order wherever books are sold

Inheritance

Aster(ix) Journal

presents

Inheritance

Summer 2019

***

Edited by
Angie Cruz

BLUE SKETCH PRESS | PITTSBURGH

See page 129 for individual copyright information/acknowledgments.

Published via Blue Sketch Press, Pittsburgh.
www.bluesketchpress.com

Inheritance
An Aster(ix) Anthology / Aster(ix) Journal
Edited by Angie Cruz—1st ed.

ISBN (print)	978-1-942547-11-2 (trade paperback)
	1-942547-11-2 (ISBN-10)

Cover art by Wura-Natasha Oguni
Cover Design by Little Owl Creative.
Copy-Edited by Joseph N. Welch III.

First Edition: September 2019

Printed in the United States of America
9 8 7 6 5 4 3 2 1

Aster(ix) Journal

www.asterixjournal.com

Aster(ix) print issues are usually published 2-3 times a year in print with additional content online. **Aster(ix)** is funded in part by the Dietrich School of Arts and Sciences and the Department of English at University of Pittsburgh.

Contents

Tender Age

Yvette Benavides

Luz always cried. Paz never did but could make others cry just by looking at them. The twin sisters grew up together, a paradox of paroxysms, in a small house with their blind grandmother, Doña Inez, an ancient woman with skin like a pecan heart, golden brown rivulets like the lines on the map of the world.

Luz could perceive the sorrows, shallow or deep, of any person and some animals and lament in loud, open wails, or tight, private, choking sobs. Once, she passed an old man on the street. Stooped over, his gait drunken and serpentine, he was a picture of desperate dignity, but moved her to spasms of tears. The old man wheezed with laugher and shook his head.

Paz could make people feel pain just by looking at them. "Duele donde mira," the people would say, meeting her gaze, wincing at the sight of her, doubling over, grabbing at their chests to loosen the tightness there, or clutching at their throats, or covering their eyes with their trembling hands. Crows fell from the sky landing with a thud at her feet after she focused on the tiny ball bearings of their eyes or admired the blueness of their black feathers. They shook off the stupor, walking sideways on spindly, twig feet. Cats yowled as if their tails were stepped on repeatedly.

Luz had always wanted a dog and found one once, a small brown, matted terrier she named Chispa. When Paz saw him, she petted him while she turned her face up to the sky to stop the eruptions of howls that came from his panting wet mouth whenever she looked into the dark eyes that drew her in to his soft, scared face. The dog whimpered, but kept wagging his tail. It was Luz's loud crying that scared him off when she was moved by the pup's act of compromise.

The girls never knew their father and their mother, Ana, died soon after childbirth. The partera informed Doña Inez of the milk leg, the "pierna de leche" that made her daughter's leg swell. It was a common enough malady among the poor mothers in Panyagua. There was no doctor in the town. This case, according to the partera and the curandera, was like nothing they had ever seen before—a leg ballooned to four times its size and covered in ulcers.

Doña Inez considered her daughter's untimely death a tender mercy. She was left to raise the girls, even with her failing eyesight.

They lived in a small house on the edge of Panyagua. It fronted the river that divided their small town with one on the other side known as Sinsueños.

From the bluff where their house stood on the edge of Panyagua, children bobbed and swam in the river. Women washed clothes, and men cast their lines for small greenish fish. Luz watched from the window sniffing back her tears and licking the saltiness of the mocos that ran into her mouth. Paz sat on the damp ground among the families wearing a big blue pañuelo over her head to cover her face. She pulled up the edge of the rag to see how big the latest catch was on the end of the fishing line of one of the men. She moved closer, catching the eye of the fish that looked at her sidewise. It bucked and fought so mightily, it snagged the line and jumped back into the murky green water of the river.

At the school, the teacher put the girls in a corner in the back of the class. Luz cried every time she saw Maestra Cleotilde and perceived her loneliness and her unquenchable thirst for a clear liquid that made her feel warm and dizzy. The teacher's breath was sour, and Luz could smell it when the teacher sighed about Paz.

"Keep that rag on your head," Maestra Cleotilde instructed Paz,"We don't want to see you! And you!" to Luz, "Stop that crying, María Magdalena!" Luz cried all the more because she knew her maestra was sad herself and spent her nights weeping into her pillow because she was a lonely spinster.

The girls were not allowed to look at the only book in the school room. It was a picture book about animals with a warped cover and brittle, wavy pages. The single time Luz and Paz were allowed to handle the book, Luz's tears drenched it to a soggy pulp. They had to leave it outside in the sun to dry to its faded, crisped condition. Maestra Cleotilde would now allow the girls to handle only a single pencil and a sheet of paper to share, and they sat in the dark corner for the whole day while the other children learned the alphabet and their numbers. The sisters could hear what they said and practiced together as best they could. Luz's tears would fall on the paper, dissolving away what they had scribbled there and making it impossible to write on without tearing it with the point of the pencil.

The children were told not to look at Paz. Luz was told not to look at the other children for fear that the fount of endless tears would distract them from their lessons. Sometimes, when Luz looked askance at the children, the tears came unbidden. Most of the children had not eaten breakfast and their thoughts of the hollows in their stomachs brought forth wails from Luz that shook the windows of the room.

One day, when a gang of wild boys approached Luz while she stood outside the school, she cried hard and inconsolably, perceiving the rough homes of the boys. She saw in full bloom in her mind the sorrows of each. This one was fatherless, this one's mother on drugs, this one had confusing feelings about the other boys. This one was chubby and felt self-conscious. This one was skeletal no matter what he ate. The gang of wild boys laughed at her, thinking at first that they had succeeded in scaring her.

"How much money do you have?" the fatherless one asked.

"I only have six pesos," she said, "but I am saving this for a book of my own I want to buy." The boys all laughed.

"Where are you gonna buy a book here in Panyagua?" asked one. He pulled out a knife and went to grab Luz's arm as she pushed her fist into the pocket of her dress. As he did so, Paz approached.

"Sister! Don't give them our pesos!" The boys turned to see Paz standing there, the pañuelo around her neck, her face exposed.

The fatherless boy fell over, his hands pressed hard against his closed eyes to give them an extra cover against what he had just seen.

"Sister!" said Luz, her mouth contorted, the tears soaking the front of her dress, "Cover your face!"

The chubby boy fell to his knees and vomited thick greenish curds. The skeletal boy rolled around in what the other threw up and howled, pounding the sidewalk with his fists. They staggered to their feet and joined the other boys, all of them running away screaming.

Luz pulled the pesos out of her pocket and waved her fist in the air offering it to anyone who would take it from her if it meant the cries and screams would stop. Paz pulled her sister's arm down and told her to be quiet.

"Sister, we cannot stay here," she said, the blue handkerchief now on her head shielding the top part of her face. "These boys will return and you will always cry when you see them and the sadness they cannot keep from your eyes, even with their daggers."

Maestra Cleotilde emerged from the door of the school.

"Niñas, you cause so much trouble. And there is no one here to help you. I wish you would go away from here." She pointed to the top of her head and Paz patted the blue rag in place. Luz cried.

When the girls went to Doña Inez with the idea that they should follow what Maestra Cleotilde said and perhaps travel to Sinsueños, she agreed. She said that in Sinsueños they could find a school or a hospital where they could get help for their odd maladies. Luz stared into her abuela's blind eyes, blued and cloudy. She could not perceive any emotion in the old woman, any feeling of sorrow or fretting. She could only sense a kind of muted hope. She sniffed and wiped her eyes.

"You must go there," said Doña Inez, her murky eyes staring past the girls. Luz blew her nose with the hem of her pinafore. "I have tried everything to help you, girls. Now you must go. There are many people there who came from someplace else, from across this river and oceans and the sky. Many people. They will know exactly how to help you. You must go now."

Luz considered her words.

"It must be true. If everyone has daddies and pesos and books why would I ever cry there? Who could I ever see that would make me feel sad?"

Paz shrugged.

"Maybe only me," she said. "Maybe I will be the only one in Sinsueños that you will feel sorry for?"

"Why you?" asked Luz. "If we go there together, we will always be happy because we will have pesos and books and each other."

The girls set out the next day on a lancha that looked like a large floating bed. They borrowed it from a fisherman's wife who took one peso from Luz, leaving her with five for the journey. They floated along in the gloom of a gray afternoon, drifting this way and that and landing on the other side of the river. It took minutes. When they were close enough to the bluff, they portaged the tiny craft and hid it in the thick impenetrable carrizo and the wild, grotesque mesquite trees that shadowed the entry of this new town.

Three uniformed people emerged from behind the thinnest part of the wall of trees and tall weeds. One yanked back the leash of a skinny, wild-eyed dog that growled and bared its yellow fangs.

"Stop!" yelled one of the officers. It was a woman with a stomach like a large drum and dyed yellow hair like straw. She wore sunglasses that made her look blind. Her heavy make-up made her skin look orange.

"You there!" she screamed at Paz. "Take that hat off!"

"You mean this?" asked Paz. "This is not really a hat. It's just a rag to cover my face." The lady officer pulled out her gun and shot it into the air. Startled, Luz pulled down Paz's rag, exposing her face to everyone. The wild-eyed, skinny dog pulled on the leash and ran away and cowered under the shade of a cypress tree. One officer fainted. One lost his balance and leaned against the fat lady officer.

Luz cried, not because she perceived emotion in the officers, but because she saw nothing at all, no emotions. The fat lady was thinking about hamburgers. The other officer was thinking about kissing the fat lady's orange face.

They took the girls into a large white building that smelled like the inside of an armpit. They saw nothing but children in grey clothing sitting in cages. Other officers banged on the cages with their open hands. "Stop crying!" they would yell as they passed each one, never looking inside the cages at the children holding their tiny arms up, calling for their mami.

By now the officers had forced Paz to wear a paper bag over her head to cover her face. They threw her into a cage and instructed her not to remove the bag. The fat lady told Luz to remove the pinafore and put on the gray uniform and then she put her hand into the pocket of the pinafore and removed the five pesos. She pushed them into the slit of her own pocket with the smallest finger of her tiny hand, all that she could squeeze into the tight pants, her long red tie hanging over the large barrel of her stomach.

Walking toward the cages, Luz looked around at the hundreds of children. All of them cried. 2000 children cried at the same time. The sound of it, and the explosion of their collective sorrows she perceived at that moment were so overwhelming, that her sadness turned to a rage that she felt for the first time in her life. It was an odd feeling—the anger and also feeling of a power or a will to suppress it at the same time. It made her feel even more exhausted than when she cried all day long.

The children cried while they slept, a winsome sound like doves cooing.

Luz spotted Paz's cage and saw her sister lying on the ground with the bag over her head.

"Did that music make you go mi-mi, Sister? Did the children's song make you go to sleep?" Paz did not move. She did not say anything.

Luz tried to put her arms through the slim bars of Paz's cage.

"Sister? Sister? Wake up, Sister! My sister! Help my sister!" Luz called out into the air. A guard approached with the wild dog.

The fat officer with the orange face entered Paz's cage "What's wrong with her?" She kicked at Paz's feet.

Another guard pulled the bag from her head. He stumbled backwards, knocking the fat orange-faced woman to the ground. All the guards ran to the cage. Dozens of them gasped and exclaimed at the sight of Paz's beauty. Many of them wept and cried out, "She is so beautiful! She is the most beautiful girl I have ever seen!"

They huddled around the girl and tried to rouse her, but it was too late.

When they turned around, Luz was gone.

The lancha was where they had left it. Luz pushed and grunted and slid it back into the water. The brown matted terrier swam toward her, paddling rhythmically. She helped it onto the boat.

The dog wagged his tail. Luz, her face streaked with salt, covered her head with her sister's blue rag, stuck her pole into the water to propel the small boat, and stared straight ahead, toward the horizon, away from Sinsueños, away, too, from Panyagua. They floated along the greenish gloaming. A silver sky opened before her, a passage free for anyone.

Pastelitos

Lorraine Avila

They were starving. All he had in his fridge was a pack of la masa y un chin de queso. It wasn't the first of the month; therefore, he hadn't been able to borrow his mother's EBT card to make compras yet. There was rice under the sink and dried beans soaking on the stove.

She was new but already proved to be the smartest girl in Julia De Burgos High. Girls like her spent their time swimming in numbers and pressing up on books. But she was also a rebel, and would cursed a teacher out without using insults but by saying what she really thought.

Boys like him were not supposed to have girls like her sitting in their living rooms.

She sat on his couch, the plastic still on it. She held onto her phone like it was a friend. He didn't know that her pupils were burning from the light on the screen, and she was trying everything not to look back at him. She had never cut school to be with a boy before. He had never cut school at all.

You cook? She pouted her lips to point at the masa on his hands.

I know how to fry pastelitos.

Pastelitos ain't no real meal.

They good though, right? He didn't know how to cook rice and beans, but he knew how to fry something quick. He bent down to pick up the canola oil and ignored the small mouse scurrying around in the dark corners of the kitchen. From the oven, he bought out the frying pan.

Pastelitos de queso, he whispered to himself, his chest proud.

Con cachu?

Siempre, he replied. She shivered at the word always. Like he wasn't just talking about a food condiment.

You cook? He asked.

No, she moved closer to where he was. She tucked her phone into her back pocket. He unwrapped the masa, and set it next to her, cut a piece of white cheese and placed it on one of the sides of the circle. He wet the fork with water. Watch me. He folded the circle in half and it cradled the piece of cheese. He then used the fork to make dents along the edges that sealed the masa. Every time he pressed down, the veins on his forearms popped and she wanted to bite into him.

Your turn, he said.

She took the lead. Perfect pastelitos on her first try.

You smart, you real smart, he smirked.

They could survive anywhere.

He twisted the cap on the stove, put the back of his hand to his hip. He thought about all of the things he could teach her to fry. Why don't you know how to cook?

My dad wanted me to focus on school.

Ven, he said. He moved closer to the stove when the oil started crackling.

Throw it in there, you can do it, he said.

¿Tu 'ta loco?

The heat kicked louder and the oil yelled. And she prayed that the oil wouldn't get her face. She slipped the uncooked pastelito into the pan and then they both hurried away, coming back only to turn the pastelito over.

When all four pastelitos were done they sat on the couch and dipped them into ketchup before biting into them. She covered her mouth and blew through her teeth.

Then they watched TV. He laughed loudly at The Office. She smirked, not sure what the joke was.

You don't get it?

No. My ESL teacher told me that it would take me a while to get jokes and metaphors in English. I've only been here eight months.

He's just stupid, he said.

Stupidity isn't funny to me anyway. She smacked her lips.

That's cause you're smart.

She only got A's in school. He didn't.

So are you, she said. He read thick books and said words her tongue could not twist to pronounce.

He smiled, twitching at his cheek. He didn't believe it but he liked to think he could be talented or smart.

During lunch periods, she wouldn't give him the time of day. He was tall and lanky and his facial hair had come too early making him look like a dork instead of a man. She hung out with her girls, and her girls hung out with the basketball team. And he was not the type to jump or run. He liked to ride horses and teach them to dance bachata with his uncles back in Santiago. But then Mr. Rubin placed them in the same math working group, and their third partner got sick with the flu. That's when they got to talk while the rest of the class caught up with how quick they did their work. That's when she told him she want to cut school and he said, I got open crib, like he had heard other boys say. She smiled—all the confirmation he needed.

They played Uno, and when she won, she got up and hollered, !Es que yo si sé de esto! And he licked his lips. She bent at her waist and kissed him holding the back of his head. His mouth was warm, and her tongue felt like a flying thing to him. When she pulled away to breathe, the shame of being all the boys his mother told him not to be settled in his chest.

We don't have to, Mari.

I want to, she held his hand. I was the one that kissed you, Ulisses. No seas palomo.

His hands found hers behind her back. His fingers became a series of magnets that stuck to her. The lingering scent of cheese on her lips. She bit him softly and before he let go, to look at this girl who had just come from the island and was all brains, he tasted his own blood.

Architecture of a *Staircase*

Rosa Boshier

11am on a Wednesday

I started the day considering the figure but soon became preoccupied with the space. At the time the figure took up most of the space. The figure of my novel was Minerva. The novel was about 70% figure. The space, when completed, I hoped would be positive—filled with palms, flamingo flowers, the aqua of Colombia's caribeño coast, inkblot skylines, life-affirming noise, the street urchins of London's mid-70s. But at that moment, the figure was floating around in mostly negative space—90/10, I would say.

The figure picked at her skin, making little maps with the excess. I bit into my erasure and wondered if this was a way she created space. At this point in the novel, her space was cross-hatched with mothers, lovers, sour looks from strangers, and, on occasion, David Bowie. Life events punctuated the space, but couldn't fully pin down the rotating settings. Minerva's skin maps were the most stable landscapes, I realized. What happened to my understanding of the figure's space when the figure reconfigured the way her body occupied it (or in this case, shed in it)? What kind of consideration should I give to the space created with skin? Should it be prioritized over snotty British mornings or pulsing Cartagena afternoons? I gnawed on the lemon peel in my tea, hoping to find an answer soon.

6pm on Halloween

As a gang of Harry Potter characters ambushed the candy bowl, I map solid spaces and implied ones in my head. Plaza Santo Domingo, Castillo San Felipe, Regent's Park, King's Road, Shepherd's Bush, the runny yellows of Cartagena yet again—she moves through all, tying half-hearted knots between them as she goes. How does Minerva gestalt her way into a home? As if on a treadmill, the earth beneath her rolls away from her.

Sloped Earth: Leaving a land of freewill to return to the palm of your motherland's iron fist. Discovering that the fist can crumble, like sand.

Sloped Earth: A disorientation. Leaving to come back. Coming back in order to get permission to leave.

How does Minerva's relegation to negative space affect her behavior? If she understands her surroundings as cut-outs of home rather than brick and mortar, then perhaps this explains her tolerance of abuse.

Our experience of an architectural space is strongly influenced by how we arrive in it.

London, 1975. The economy buckles. Anyone who speaks another language is politely asked to leave the post office. The Sex Pistols are turning their grimy heads inside Punk's sticky womb. When Minerva arrives she notes a light drizzle watering the pink mohawks and shaved heads that dot Chalk Farm Road. She is wearing a cream dress.

8am on a Tuesday

I woke up considering the literary feng shui of my novel en-route. Am

I willing to relinquish style for authentic voice? I revved up to rewrite a chapter in first person. It struck me as a human but not as the mother of the text. I'm not ready to hand over Minerva's vocal chords to her yet. My punishment is that she hasn't talked to me for days.

3am in a dark room

I fell asleep pressing my ear to a pile of poems. I plucked them from the spine of a book and laid them at the top of my bed like pillows. I wadded more and more sheets on top of each other, separating each poem with colored tissue paper so that they shone like embers in the dark. When I had built a nest for my head I lay it upon the poems. My ear crinkled the paper. I thought I heard the poems whisper to me. At night, I felt the surge of words absorbed into my body. I woke up with language.

My day's target was the poem. My route: the reading chair to the kitchen table to the bathroom, repeat. I had created my poem pillow to insert reward into my path. Sleep was a necessary path. I thought that lining sleep with tools that could encourage my target, yet disabling my ability to engage with them, might strike a rich balance of denial and reward. Enough to let language come to me like tightrope walkers—slow and precarious, but coming.

I wanted to protect them and to honor their journey, so I wrote very slowly. I cradled each one, eking it out like the letters in a second-grader's cursive journal. One by one, like beads of water rolling down a car window, they came. All but the last one. I wondered what I must deny to coax it out.

4pm in Los Angeles

I'm deciding if Minerva is the novel's foundation, or just an attic window. Does she support or crown the novel? Will she continue to be a receptacle, or will she create her own container? Will she break out of the container that people place her in? Switching the label from *spare linens* to *childhood toys*? I know each room holds a journey—through continents, in and out of affections and youth movements. Minerva is at the base of herself, the base of society, the base of culture burgeoning, but she can't hold the book up by herself.

Minerva and her mother Valeria hold everything together. If Minerva is my base then Valeria is my roof. Valeria has the potential to either topple or adorn. She will do both. Her arc of descent is exquisite in its annihilation.

9pm on a Friday outside of Starbucks

I leave and promise myself I'll come back because Valeria is not coming to me. When I strike her like a bell, only tin resounds. She takes no shape outside of her anger and addiction. Inflated by them, she's too easy to puncture.

Outside I see a sports car with no permit parked in a handicapped spot—a visual representation of fragility. Whatever foundation they wake up in every day cannot be solid.

1pm on a Thursday

In the downtown office of the urban planning nonprofit I work at, we debate about the front door's relationship to the wall.

10:30am on a Sunday when it is raining

I started the day hiking with a friend in Cherry Canyon. The dusty trails were wet and looked like sweaty camels. The landscape sighed as we progressed upon it. Our shoes became soggy from the mud path we mound up, thickening the further we walked. The flat smoke of the sky twisted and curled above us.

My painter friend felt she was groping in the dark. She had just completed a show that had given her nothing except a feeling of being intact, which was in fact everything. She asked me what we do as artists who can feel completed by acts that seem to do nothing—they have not resolved a social issue, they have not brought us money or fame—but they feel like a further wrinkle in the right brain, and this wrinkle has a healing property. The wrinkle tightens around our understanding of how we wish to move in this world. I tell her that I'm just going to keep following the folds. I'll keep folding and folding until one day, maybe, I'll have a fucking paper crane.

10am, November 11th, 2016

Two days ago, America elected a reality TV star and sex predator as its next president. How does he fit into my intercontinental family portrait? The distance of placing xenophobia in the 1970s, 5,000 miles away, feels like an indulgence. I am reminded of a quote: *Cowardice is a form of decadence.* My book feels like chocolate cake.

Has the U.S. performed a form of decadence? Our president elect is famous for yelling *You're fired!* at budding entrepreneurs. He's also the face of WrestleMania. He now has control of my ovaries.

I received frantic emails from friends asking me about where to get an IUD. *What if I want kids before the end of this presidency? Where can I take it out?* I want to engulf them in my maze of positive and negative space. Build a home for them that way. Lock the new president out of the architecture of my fiction. Make this our new reality.

November 14, 2016

What is the architecture of this cowardice? Conservatives throw pebbles at the veil of diversity in the White House. The curtain sighs a little. But white Liberals laid the bricks. We wrongly believed "our" work was now done. Conservative America built upon this cowardice, using the belief, posited by the left, that our black president would resolve our social disparities as cement. Conservatives were just fortifying the liberal staircase.

We built the foundation and they shellacked the walls with textured fears of the "Other." Gradients of economic concerns, fear of losing social security, an allergy to Spanish, an affection for the Confederate flag. Liberals constructed the house and Conservatives decorated. Like a fussy old couple we fought about the end product.

How have Valeria and Minerva performed cowardice? Valeria's was enacted in abuse. Silence hardened her. She could not be persuaded of compassion's cooling powers. Minerva allowed abuse to linger like her shadow until it caught her. Only then did she perform an exorcism. A space erects around her that she must then blow apart.

On a morning in which Winter warmed into Spring

I used to think inspiration would strike when I wandered into the unknown—a foreign city, a grand landscape, a strange romance. It's easy to follow the impulse to write these encounters, but how do I write the familiar? Often times I shy away from it. It is too close to me. It gives the uncomfortable friction of a second skin—not quite on me but gently covering—somehow just out of reach.

November 2, 2017

I decided on eggs instead of cereal and mulled over the possibility of the colonial conscious scaffolding the novel. But I'm old-fashioned, and feel like I need a body to put to my narrator. How do I invite in a voice that already has its tongue on everything? It reminds me of the oil in *Fern Gully*. It comes hissing down, permeating everything.

November 3, 2017

I began the day thinking about what form this hissing consciousness would take. What formal constraints would it have? My professor suggested a hybrid screenplay/novel, but I'm not sure I want to give the oil another lens.

November 5, 2017

I began typing Juan's voice, Minerva's childhood best friend. Previously, he had been a pillar, but as I cast an eye across my landscape of characters, I wondered, is he not the pure embodiment of colonized thinking? A rich brat from the Walled City with socialist fancies who tries to peel off his opulent skin by joining los guerrilleros? Who wriggles back into the pelt of privilege when things get tough, and wouldn't you know, it still fits him just fine. Who else to talk back at assumptions of class in European immigration patterns? Who knows the figure better than he?

2:30pm, Sunday, almost mid-November

I tentatively made additions. Adding a stone here, a high beam there. Then I got ambitious and began lobbing on extra rooms, a trembling third story. The extra rooms were filled with characters I cared about but that I was not sure were connected to the foundation of the novel. The novel started to tilt sideways and slide down the hillside. I weighed it down with a garage. I worry the house may split open from being dragged in two directions.

A Thursday evening, December

The success of the masterpieces seems to lie not so much in their freedom from faults—indeed we tolerate the grossest errors in them all—but in the immense persuasiveness of a mind which has completely mastered its perspective.

—Virginia Woolf, "The Death of the Moth"

I have built a house that groans under its own weight. It's a house filled with cracks that mice slip in and out of. Wind blows through it like a shape-shifting ghost. The house rattles with every haunting shriek. But at least I know where the silverware is kept.

The One-Eyed Bat!

Yalitza Ferreras

The guy I'm dating in Ann Arbor is The One-Eyed Bat! He wrestles with a mask over one eye. He's from a Mayflower family in Massachusetts, and he goes to Mexico to wrestle Lucha Libre-style. He jumps from the ropes onto his opponents and ensnares them with his black velvet bat wings. It's an art thing.

When he drives us to Detroit, to photograph urban ruins, we pass this wiener sign outside the factory where they make them on Holbrook Street. The wiener is in big red neon, disproportionate in size to the building it is attached to by a giant skewer. The first time I saw the sign, I gasped and screamed out, A big red wiener! and he just nodded as the wiener cast its shadow on us, didn't even crack a smile. The wiener sign says "Kowalski" and is in the city of Hamtramck, just outside of Detroit. Has there ever been a more delightful name for a city? H-A-M-T-R-A-M-C-K. It needs more vowels. I think about the missing vowels, and phonemes and epenthesis, and I think that Hamtramck seems like enough when you say the name, but not when you see the word. Sometimes he takes my left hand in his and blows warmth into it as we drive on ice-covered streets, and I feel happy. The first time he took me to Ypsilanti for another art thing, and we approached the city's old water tower, named the Word's Most Phallic Building by entities that declare such things, I didn't say anything as we drove by its girthy base on Summit Street, the highest point in the city. He was talking about the themes of masculinity in his Lucha Libre project. Summit Street! I was hoping he would notice the delight on my face, but he didn't. Okay, so I try to engage with his work, I say, uropatagium instead of fixating on penis. We talk about studies on how bats use their uropatagia in flight thrust, but when I call the membrane their bat butts, I lose him. So anyway, what scientists are saying is that wings are obvious, but bat butts are important, too.

And then we get to Detroit, and he makes art. I wander around the decay of these abandoned buildings, and I politely ease out of his frame, spinning on split floorboards, risking my life on tippy toes. He takes these photographs that make the desolation look like a movie set built just for him to explore themes of loss of industry and people. After elegiac pronouncements, he lights the shot, makes use of something that was once useful. Then, we fuck.

I am supposed to be writing. He's a multi-medium artist. I don't mean multi-media. He sings and plays guitar and dances and takes pictures, and he mentioned something about a unicycle once, and he makes films, and this wrestling thing too. He must've exhausted his parents. My mother says that I was sometimes so quiet she had to poke me to make sure I was okay.

I walk around. I don't understand why everyone is in love with these ruins. I prefer the parts of Detroit with people in them. All of these places look like my childhood memories of burned out squats in Bushwick, where I was born brown like everyone around me, you know, before Bushwick was cool. Detroit feels familiar, but this is not my city, these are not my ruins. He is photographing a heap of books with mushrooms growing out of them. These dead books are my worst nightmare. I am standing off to the side under an art-deco archway, its red, blue and orange tiles fallen off and strewn at my feet. A faint light glows through a hole in the floor. I take a step forward, and a loud clanging echoes through the space. He looks up and tells me to be careful, and I think about pressing down harder. I want to make an offering to this place. I picture my congealed guts dangling off the jagged entrails of the building. I slide down carefully instead. I put down a knee. Other knee. Head tilts. I slowly uncoil my scarf from around my neck. I call him over.

Afterwards, we go to the gallery in Detroit where he's showing the photographs of himself soaring above Mexicans in his flappy wings, black shorts and Lucha Libre mask. In one image, he stands on the ropes of a makeshift boxing ring outdoors in a field or what looks like someone's backyard. He is gritting his teeth, stomach muscles bulging. He is beautiful. His tousled white-blond hair is peeking out of the half-face head mask that makes him The One-Eyed Bat! His body looks like a classical statue looming over his opponents.

They say that bats see better than humans. What I see is the torso from a David about to topple on all these smaller, rounder, browner men, but I don't say it. I start waving my hands around the space. I tell him what I think about the lighting, how to arrange the photographs, not what I think about white bodies coming down on brown bodies in their own backyards. The gallery owner comes over and smiles at me like, you guys are such a great couple. I just keep trying to make some arrangement out of the pieces and pointing at the walls.

Tender Birria

Myriam Gurba

[A NOTE FROM THE AUTHOR: As my lesbian marriage was disintegrating, I experimented with dating men and writing letters to the dead. I wrote one to Gertrude Stein nearly every day in order to see if it would make Alice B. Toklas mad. What follows are some of the results.]

"…it was not natural to have come from there yes write about it if I like or anything if I like but not there, there is no there there…"

Gertrude Stein

"Smoke weed everyday."

Alice B. Toklas

Dear Gertrude,

I don't have to introduce myself to you. You already know everything there is to know about me. You have this insight because I'm communicating to you through the Ouija board of my mind. Often, people compare the mind to a machine or computer. John Locke referred to it as a tabula rasa. Ancient Greeks conceived of it as wax tablet. I reject those analogies. I prefer the notion of it as an occult instrument.

The day suicide bombers attacked the Bataclan, killing fans during an Eagles of Death Metal concert, I went to hang out with my friends Lenny and Lydia. Medical marijuana smoke fogged their living room. Lydia lazed on the sectional. A box lazed in her lap.

After sliding off its lid, Lydia pulled out the Ouija board and set it on the coffee table. Lenny and I sat cross-legged on the floor, facing each other across the board. It was our investigative tool. We'd decided to use it to get to the bottom of things in France. Terrorists had already claimed responsibility for the attacks but nobody was left to describe what it had felt like to die during the siege and we wanted to know what it felt like to be enjoying an American band in Paris and then die. Was there a moment of existential anxiety before death? Does existential anxiety persist into the afterlife? How does one experience irony in the French afterlife? We would find out.

Lydia found a Sesame Street style program in French on YouTube. Children's voices chanted simple sentences, simple enough for me to decipher after three years of French in Catholic high school.

Vanilla candles burned. Their flames provided the only light in the house.

The cat, Ugly, sat by the heater. She watched.

Lenny and I placed our fingers on the planchette.

"Bonjour," I began. "French spirits, are you here?"

The planchette glided to

O…

U…

I.

Have you ever noticed that the French word for yes is IOU's anagram?

"How many of there are you?" I asked.

The piece glided to 1.

"Ghost…" I said. "Are you gay?"

The planchette flew to YES.

"Ghost…are you single?"

The shade clumsily guided the planchette, spelling out that she was a lesbian bachelor "living" on a houseboat. After teasing us with that, she quit answering our questions.

Gertrude, please don't be like that French lesbian ghost. Talk to me. I worship your face. I worship your hubris. Your hubris validates mine.

Dear Gertrude,

I am mostly Mexican but I'm also part Polish. Your face looked like my Polish great great grandma's. I think of her as a babushka even though that's a Russian thing. I think of you as a babutchka since you seem maternal and paternal at the same time.

Dear Gertrude,

The French are nuts. A French woman was the first patient in cosmetic history to receive a partial face transplant. The woman had tried to commit suicide and while unconscious, her Labrador Retriever ate some of her. To fix her, doctors sewed on a new face that had belonged to a woman who had killed herself.

That is so French.

I watched the suicide survivor appear on TV wearing the suicide victim. She sat at a table, speaking into a microphone, smoking. That couldn't have been good for her new face. Which was somebody else's old face. Shabby chic. It seems very French to get a new face sewn on and then ruin it with cigarettes. So cavalier. So French.

Dear Gertrude,

I'm going to put my name inside you. Gurbtrude.

Dear Gertrude,

A Rosie O'Donnell is a Rosie O'Donnell is a Rosie O'Donnell is a

Rosie O'Donnell.

Dear Gertrude,

Here is a text exchange about you.

Me to a lover
Who was the
Last person to
Fist me:
There's no tender
button emoji.

The fister's reply:
I ♥ this text.
Texts are somehow
perfect for reaching
the tender buttons.

Dear Gertrude,

If your middle name was Pendeja, your initials would be GPS.

Dear Gertrude,

"Pendeja" is the feminine form of pendejo. It's used to mean dummy and it's pretty harsh. Although it's used to communicate how idiotically a person is behaving, what it actually means is "pube."

Dear Gertrude,

In Spanish, your name is Gertrudis. That reminds me of clitoris.

Dear Gertrude,

You wrote, "America is my country and Paris is my hometown."

You are such a fucking snob.

So am I.

Dear Gertrude,

I hate the Red Hot Chili Peppers.

Dear Gertrude,

My heart wears a beret. Here's why.

When I was little, before my brother and sister were born, before I knew how to read, before I could walk, before everything, my parents took me to McDonald's.

Mom and I watched Dad order our food and carry it over. He set our tray down in the middle of our table, and before any many, woman, or child could, French fries seduced me. They smelled perfect. I lunged at them. I had to. I wanted them. My tiny fingers grabbed. They ripped fries from their sack and made a fist around them. Steam curled. Grease burned my palm. I wailed. I moaned, "French fry!" In my mind, French fry and Joan of Arc are inseparable.

"Let go!" screamed Dad. He reached to rip the fries out of my fist. I moaned, "French fry!" and brought my fist close to my heart.

I was willing to tolerate pain for possession.

I wailed French fry before I said mother, father, or anything else that mattered. French fry was my first word. That is so American. McDonald's is my hometown. Ronald McDonald is my president. I speak French. Anyone who orders fries in America does.

Dear Gertrude,

There is a horrible place named HomeTown Buffet. I went there on Mother's Day with my grandmother.

She devoured four plates of mashed potatoes and meatloaf before making her final trip back to the buffet. She returned with a plate full of fried chicken. She shrouded a breast, a wing, and a thigh in white napkins and shoved them in her purse. My wife stared as fowl disappeared. Realizing she was being watched, my grandmother quit meat packing. She made eye contact with my wife. She still had some drumsticks left to deal with.

In a tone that suggested that the obvious required explanation, my grandmother said, "Its for the dogs." My grandmother is both Mexican and dead. Someday I will be part-Mexican and dead.

Next door to HomeTown Buffet stands another buffet, Souplantation. I like eating there because there are a lot of fresh vegetables but I find its antebellum name troubling. I steal their apples and muffins like my mom taught me to. I never steal meat or soup. I hate soup anyways. I prefer a meal you can chew.

Dear Gertrude,

What meat do you carry in your purse?

Dear Gertrude,

There isn't a larger point to this. That's what makes talking to you fun. I can tell you whatever. When I was growing up, my mom wouldn't let me answer "whatever." She thought that was very rude and very American.

For example, if she were to have asked me, «¿Quieres espagueti para la comida?» and I was to have answered, "Whatever," she would've gotten pissed. She never slapped me for answering "whatever." My mom only attacked me once, when I told her that when it came to Nietzsche, he was right about god. I guess she did also attack me when I screamed at her that when I was fourteen, during a blackout, a boy raped me and took my underwear.

We were sitting on my bed, sharing the underwear detail triggered the hyperventilation, and I didn't even see her hand. I just felt it smack my face.

It cured my hyperventilation.

Calmly, I asked her, "Why did you hit me?"

"So that you would calm down," she answered in Spanish.

Mom usually speaks to me in Spanish.

I answer in English.

We have a bilingual relationship.

Dear Gertrude,

Whatever. Whatevs.

Dear Gertrude,

The rudest thing I ever did was thread erect needles onto a man's chair. I was ten. Once he sat down, I realized that perhaps I'd made a mistake.

Dear Gertrude,

Your name has rude in it.

Dear Gertrude,

This isn't an epistolary novel. I learned about epistolary novels in high school. There's something very urinary about the word epistolary. It makes me think of the color yellow. The first book I heard described as epistolary was *Dracula*. In high school, I really liked the book *Griffin and Sabine*. It wasn't just epistolary, it had actual envelopes in it that you could open and tease letters out of and unfold and read. It felt voyeuristic to participate in its world. In college, I read my roommate's mail. I steamed it open using a tea kettle. When I was finished, I glued the envelopes back shut and put them back on the shelf where I'd found them. Reading other people's mail, especially when it comes from prison, is one of the most thrilling things in the world. So is vandalizing the vehicles of Pro-Life activists.

Dear Gertrude,

Sometimes I think my gender is coffee. Sometimes I think my gender is art. Sometimes I think my gender is California.

Dear Gertrude,

I first read your stuff in college.

I hated it.

Dear Gertrude,

I used to watch this TV show called *In Living Color*. It was an urban sketch comedy show and one of the recurring sketches involved Blaine and Antoine, two black fags who reviewed movies from a "men's point of view." Their show was called Men on Film. Anytime they reviewed a movie with muscle bound guys, they loved it. Antoine described Deliverance as a film about love and camping. Blaine used two words to describe movies he loved: Scrum. Shuss.

Anytime a movie featured women, Blaine and Antoine chorused, "Hated it!"

Anytime a movie featured lots of women, they chorused, "Double hated it!"

Gertrude Stein, that's how I felt about your work when I first read it.

Double hated it.

It's *so* filled with the presence of women.

Dear Gertrude,

I imagine that there's a graveyard for unanswered text messages in outer space. Letters float through it. Most of the letters are Ws, Ys, and Ds. D is shorthand for dick. My gynecologist told me I have a vitamin

D deficiency.

Dear Gertrude,

You wrote that there is no there there about your real home town, Oakland.

I lived there once, in an apartment by a gay bar called the White Horse.

I met my wife at the White Horse. She was a white butch and she bought me a bottle of Budweiser. I sipped it and looked at her. Over techno music, she screamed, “Are you Mexican?”

“Yes!” I screamed back.

She screamed, “I love Selena!”

Usually, when people say stuff like that to me, I want to kill them. Since I was sexually attracted to her, I let it slide. We danced to techno music. She took me for a spin on her motorcycle. We moved in together.

Pink carpeted our apartment. Our ceiling was slanted. From our front balcony, we could see the feminist bookstore across the street. I got in trouble there. At the front counter, I asked an employee, “You guys have any bell hooks?”

The employee glanced to her right. Then, she glanced to her left.

She growled, and I mean growled, “I don’t see any guys around here.”

She wouldn’t answer my question until I castrated it.

Dear Gertrude,

My girlfriend was asleep. Larry was over. We had the Ouija between us. We sat on the pink carpet. We touched the movable piece.

Larry said, “Dad, I miss you.”

I felt sad. To me, we were playing a game. To Larry, this was real.

Dear Gertrude,

In my third grade classroom, a framed poster of The Starry Night hung by the door. I didn't know Van Gogh had painted it. I thought maybe an amateur, like my grandma, had painted it. When I was bored, I'd stare at it and think, "I could do better."

Which is not to say that I think I'm better than you. I do, however, recreationally rewrite your work. I also have my own interpretation of your work. For example, I believe your phrase *a spectacle and nothing strange* is about my gay cousin Sergio. I believe that "A RED STAMP" which goes *if lilies are lily white if they exhaust noise and distance and even dust, if they dusty will dirt a surface that has no extreme grace, if they do this and it is not necessary it is not necessary at all necessary if they do this they need a catalogue* is about white people. I believe that *a sad size a size that is not sad is blue as every bit of blue is precocious* is about Viagra.

In the beginning of the FOOD section of Tender Buttons, there's sort of a table of contents of all the things you write about: ROASTBEEF; MUTTON; BREAKFAST; SUGAR; CRANBERRIES; MILK; EGGS; APPLE; TAILS; LUNCH; CUPS; RHUBARB; SINGLE; FISH; CAKE; CUSTARD; POTATOES; ASPARAGUS; BUTTER; END OF SUMMER; SAUSAGES; CELERY; VEAL; VEGETABLE; COOKING; CHICKEN; PASTRY; CREAM; CUCUMBER; DINNER; DINING; EATING; SALAD; SAUCE; SALMON; ORANGE; COCOA; AND CLEAR SOUP AND ORANGES AND OAT-MEAL; SALAD DRESSING AND AN ARTICHOKE; A CENTRE IN A TABLE.

My version goes: RANCH DRESSING; TORTILLAS; CAPTAIN CRUNCH; LEAN CUISINE; PAN DULCE; EATING OVER THE SINK; NON-DAIRY CREAMER; COFFEE; COFFEE; COFFEE; SLEEP-EATING WHILE ON AMBIEN SORT OF ANOREXIC; ALKA SELTZER; CORN DOGS; BLOOD ORANGES; PEANUT BUTTER TRAIL MIX; PLAIN YOGURT; SHOPLIFTING FROM WHOLE FOODS; ASSPARAGUS; LITE ICE CREAM; BUTTER;

CHOCOLATE-FILLED CROISSANT; HEIRLOOM TOMATOES; ORGANIC PINK LADIES; RAISINETTES; FOOD FIGHTS; I HATE SOUP.

Gertrude, have you heard of bibliomancy? It's a form of divination where you ask a question of the universe and then find the answer buried in the Bible. The poetry form of it is called rhapsodomancy. I used rhapsodomancy to answer a question. I asked, "Should I get breast implants?" and I opened *Tender Buttons.* Guess which poem I opened to? "CUPS." I read *a single example of excellence is in the meat* and *a cup is neglected by being full of size.* I took this as a *yes* to my question so when people ask if I got breast implants I say *yes.* When they ask why, I answer, "Poetry."

I might be crazy.

Here is a rewrite I did of your poem "ASPARAGUS."

ASSPARAGUS

Assparagus in a lean in a lean to hot. You pee and it smells interesting. This makes it art and it is wet wet weather we weather wet.

Your version is more literary but my version is more fun. It's hard to be fun and literary. But it's also the best.

You summarize my eating habits with your poem "SALAD." It is a winning cake.

In my copy of Tender Buttons, I wrote SH next to the title of the third section of the book, "ROOMS."

Some people like to do drugs before they write. I'm not really into that.

Dear Gertrude,

I think I would've made a good heroin addict but I feel like it's too late for that.

ABURA

Ángela Hernández Nuñez

Saludó y dijo que estaba sediento. ¿Podíamos hacerle el favor de darle agua? Me apresuré a coger un vaso, anticipándome a Sabina. Por mi mente cruzó un celaje: ella estaba esperándolo, aunque no se hubieran visto antes. Caminé hacia la cocina, vigilando. A mi regreso estuve segura de que se habían comunicado. Él, terminando de tomarse el agua, dijo: "Permítame dejarle unas cuantas coca colas". No tiene por qué, contesté, agregando que no había nevera donde enfriarlas. Sin embargo, logró lo que buscaba, mi hija le devolvía la sonrisa. "Cuando usted vuelva por aquí nos regala los refrescos", comentó ella, pasando por alto mi respuesta.

Sabina fue mi último embarazo, mi nidal. Nació liviana como un lagarto, con el reflejo de mamar muy débil, por lo que tenía que apretarme el seno y dejarlo gotear encima de su boquita. Hasta los tres meses, evité verla desnuda entera.

Cumplidos los cinco años, Higinio, nuestro padre, la llevó al pueblo de San Juan para tomarse una fotografía con ella. Él se afanó en que mamá la alfabetizara y le enseñara los números que ella sabía. A nosotros, en cambio, desde que mudamos los dientes, Higinio nos machacaba a golpes, obligándonos a bajar el lomo y a sembrar hasta en cascajales. Nos ponía a caminar en las tinieblas y en los ventarrones. Así se cría instinto para evadir una cuchillada y aguante para trabajar en cualquier situación y terreno.

De pequeña, Sabina vivía encaramándose en los palos. Como pesaba poco, podía trepar por las palmas o columpiarse en una rama del mango. No es que fuera ruda, al contrario, sus brazos eran como de carne de jaiba, y sus ojos relucían como cogollos de pino. Sin embargo, sus problemas tenía.

A muchos niños inquietos les coge con comer tierra. En lugar de eso, nuestra única hermana, escondida debajo del piso, masticaba y tragaba flores. Una vez, Octavia, nuestra madre, tuvo que correr con ella al hospital porque el vientre se le hinchó y presentó convulsiones. El médico pensó que se había comido una planta o semillas con tóxicas. ¿Tuatúa? ¿Jabilla? ¿Brusca? ¿Mantequilla? Nadie sabía decir qué comió la niña. El doctor le practicó un lavado de estómago. Para quitarle el vicio de comer flores, nuestra preocupada madre le mezcló el horrible purgante de jalapa con cayenas machacadas y al otro día la obligó a masticar pétalos de rosa que había hervido con cañafístula, el peor sabor que conocemos. Papá desaprobaba ese método. A escondidas, compensaba a Sabina con caramelos.

Una noche, transcurrido un mes luego de la intoxicación, soñamos que Sabina pintaba los árboles del patio con colores de agua en medio de fuertes brisas. Y que todo lo que traía el viento, fuera cucaracha o escarabajo, sapo o alacrán, en chocando con los troncos, se ablandaba y era asimilado por la corteza. Octavia e Higinio, desde sus sillas, contemplaban indolentes y a gusto la actividad de su hija mimada. Los hermanos, que la soñábamos a una, en el sueño dormíamos desentendidos.

Sin sospechar lo que ocasionaría, al poco tiempo, ya próximo el Día de la Madre, le trajimos a Octavia una hermosa planta de lirios, crecida en la zona más fría de la montaña. En el centro de cada flor, se erigía como un pequeño dedo, cubierto de polvo amarillo solar. Sabina llegó a comerse dos, escapando despavorida, con la lengua afuera, como si le hubieran estrujado fogaraté en la misma. Tenía los labios y el paladar repletos de marquitas sangrientas y le palpitaba la garganta. Lloró durante horas. Este suceso fue en verdad el que la curó de masticar flores metida debajo del piso de madera.

En ocasión de su primer período, la soñamos chapoteando en el arroyo. Nubes escarlatas se reflejaban entre sus piernas. Anochecía en el sueño. En la oscuridad, Sabina continuaba echándose agua como si tratara de desprenderse dura costra invisible. Al amanecer, los hermanos nos miramos en silencio mientras bebíamos el café. En el sueño siguiente, tres días después, vimos a Sabina cubierta de pintas, la piel como tela de arroz con coco, deslizándose sobre un yaguacil con los brazos en cruz y los cabellos al aire. De toda ella salía aserrín. Respiramos aliviados con el final del sueño: nuestra hermana aterrizaba en un charco de agua cristalina. Al poco, a Sabina le atacó el sarampión y en una semana se le complicó con una pulmonía. "No se preocupe mamá. Descuide, papá. No es menester llevarla al hospital", les asegurábamos a nuestros padres. Y en efecto, de las dos enfermedades se recobró nuestra única hermana. Por entonces, ya nos habíamos acostumbrado a avistarla en el fondo de nuestro sueño; inmóvil, casi siempre. Cuando ella protagonizaba alguna acción, nosotros vigilábamos; al despertar nos sentíamos exhaustos. Por suerte, ocurría rara vez. El mismo día que ella cumplió dieciocho años, soñamos un acontecimiento que nos cubrió de un sudor frío. Al amanecer, mientras bebíamos nuestro café, nos miramos pávidos. Las manos y los labios nos temblaban. Salimos embalados a trabajar.

(El cutis de Sabina exhibe líneas, como trazadas con una pizca de añil. Por la punta de su nariz empieza un suave canal que ahueca ligeramente su barbilla y desemboca en su ombligo).

Hermógenes (no nos sorprendió su nombre), el distribuidor de refrescos embotellados volvió, claro que volvió. A cada paso, a cada gesto, se esforzaba por exhibir sus buenas intenciones hacia Sabina. En su tercera visita, le trajo un presente a nuestra hermana y no se lo entregó hasta obtener el consentimiento de Higinio para ello. A cabo de unos meses, acudió a nuestro hogar acompañado de su madre. Fue un día largo, que Hermógenes aprovechó para formalizar su propuesta de compromiso, mientras su madre le respaldaba en todo con exquisita amabilidad urbana. A cada rato, la mujer de Santo Domingo soltaba un cumplido: "Su cocina parece una tacita de oro", le decía a Octavia. "Qué aire más puro se respira aquí". "Cuántos árboles frutales. Hay que ser muy trabajador para sacarle partido a esta tierra". Nosotros nos replegamos, callados, sin interés en salvar la distancia. Higinio, fumaba su pipa y buscaba qué hacer, orgulloso e intimidado a un tiempo. A la hora del almuerzo, papá dijo que unos potrillos estaban acabando con la siembra de maíz. Todos nosotros quisimos acompañarlo, escapar de allí, pero bastó una mirada de Octavia (¡atrévanse a irse!) para inmovilizarnos.

Nosotros, descorazonados, no sabíamos qué hacer. Y se nos notaba. Sabina, en cambio, lucía radiante. Pese a nuestra mala cara, al regresar del trabajo, ella nos recibía contenta, con una ponchera de agua fresca y un lienzo al hombro. Y mientras nos contemplaba lavarnos las manos y rociarnos el pecho, nos ponía al tanto de los menudos sucesos domésticos. El color castaño se le agitaba en los ojos. En nuestro interior nos decíamos: ¿Por qué maldito destino tiene que marcharse con ese fulano del camión si aquí cuenta con diez hombres que la adoran?

Vigilábamos, qué más podíamos hacer. Espiábamos las conversaciones con su prometido, deseosos de que el hombre cometiera algún yerro. Higinio había perdido el sosiego. Él ignoraba la razón, pero su instinto de padre apegado a la hija le sugería algo vago, extraño e inquietante. Por cualquier "quítame esta paja", nos soltaba una reprimenda. Durante el desayuno, a veces, se le aguaban los ojos.

Me preguntaba qué viento había empujado a Hermógenes hasta nuestra casa. Qué sabía él de Sabina. Nosotros sí la conocíamos de veras. Le habíamos llevado el alimento a la boca y la habíamos acurrucado cuando de pequeñita la atacaban calenturas. La habíamos acompañado en su debilidad y en su fortalecimiento, desde que era menester sostenerle la cabecita para evitar que se doblara, hasta que sus piernas se volvieron recias y nos ganaba echando carreras. Cada uno de nosotros la había estrechado en sus brazos hasta dormirla.

"Vamos a vivir en un sitio cómodo", nos comunicaba Hermógenes con una sonrisa de oreja a oreja. Y mirándonos como si con sus ojos amables quisiera decirnos: Les comprendo, comprendo sus recelos de hermanos, pero no se preocupen yo la voy a cuidar y a proteger. Octavia le prestaba atención por toda la familia; escuchaba con interés cada frase que profería y cada idea sobre el futuro. A nuestra madre le simpatizaba el joven y se lo hacía saber. Eso nos hizo creer a nosotros durante meses. Ella era reservada y sabía controlar sus emociones.

Averiguaba, como al descuido, sobre sucesos y quebrantos en la familia de Hermógenes. Él me parecía demasiado pálido, como si todo el tiempo sintiera algo de frío. Sus labios tiraban al morado, había oído que así se ven las personas que padecen del corazón. Pero él no cometía falta, se comportaba con corrección y respeto, tampoco lograba sacarle informaciones sospechosas. Su madre era mujer fuerte y educada, lo habíamos comprobado; el padre, vivía en Venezuela y también las hermanas. El muchacho no tenía hijos en la calle, ni había estado interno en hospitales. Tampoco se había metido en líos de justicia. ¿Por qué no me podía sacar la espinita del corazón?

Para ganar tiempo, convencí a mi hija de que tejer cubrecamas, bordar manteles y coser la ropa que usaría de recién casada era un requisito para la buena estrella del matrimonio. Hermógenes, aunque con un poquito de tristeza, porque él prefería una rápida unión matrimonial, aceptó la contrapropuesta de Higinio de "darnos chance para prepararnos, ya que la celebración corre a cargo de los padres de la novia". El comprometido no disimulaba su congoja, cuando poníamos reparos a su intención de llevarse a Sabina a vivir a la Capital. Una semana antes de la fecha acordada, murió mi padre en un campo de Oviedo, donde se había apartado desde los tiempos de la dictadura. Dije que Sabina no podía desposarse estando nuestro hogar de luto. Ella contestó que nunca en su vida había visto a su abuelo. No era propio de mi hija contradecirme. Hubo un nuevo aplazamiento.

Llegada la nueva fecha convenida, ya no había qué más inventar para aplazar el matrimonio. A fin de cuentas, valiéndose nada más de un sueño no puede uno torcer el destino.

(El calor de Sabina despliega hormigas de alas, como el presagio de lluvia. El calor de Sabina se mueve hacia quien sienta frío. Sus pechos son como de pulpa de guayaba. Su espalda parece de palmito).

Higinio, taciturno, se escudaba en su mal humor. Mamá porfiaba con sus emociones, pero no dejaba de realizar las faenas necesarias al pie de la letra. Había preparado con celo el baño que la novia debía tomar. Ese día, siete tinajas alineadas en el patio recibieron sol desde el amanecer. Seis estaban llenas con agua del manantial, más los elementos siguientes: en la número uno, miel de abejas y sal; en la dos, cundeamor; en la tres, flores de azahar; en la cuatro, trozos de alcanfor; en la cinco, rosas blancas, rojas, amarillas y rosadas; en la sexta, hojas de menta y eucalipto. El contenido de la última tinaja, con el que Sabina debía realizar el enjuague final de su cuerpo, era el resultado de recoger el rocío nocturno en treinta vasijas durante treinta días. El líquido solo llenaba la tercera parte de la tinaja. Octavia misma se encargó de bañar a Sabina. Nosotros, de soslayo, seguíamos la operación, llevada a cabo en el cuarto sin puertas, situado cerca de la casa. Ignoramos de dónde sacó nuestra madre la idea de que ese baño riguroso protegería a su hija una vez esta abandonara la seguridad de nuestro hogar.

¿Y si aquel sueño fuera engañoso, una suerte de trampa contra la felicidad de Sabina? Octavia con tantas encomiendas y tareas no nos dejaba tiempo para pensar, como a propósito. "Todo el mundo ha de quedar contento. Que nadie encuentre qué criticar de la boda de su hermana", nos decía. Durante la celebración, nos esmeramos en atenciones a los invitados, sobre todo a los que vinieron de Santo Domingo a acompañar a Hermógenes. Por breves momentos, éramos presa de golpes de zozobra que nos hacían correr el sudor por la frente y buscarnos los ojos. Papá no consiguió sobreponerse a su malestar. Se movía de aquí para allá como un zombi. Los visitantes más observadores dieron por seguro que estaba enfermo. Ni la energía de Octavia logró sacarlo de su estado taciturno, resignado y ausente. "Es que Sabina es su vida. Y se le va a cientos de kilómetros", lo excusaba Octavia ante personas allegadas a nuestra familia.

En los días que siguieron a la partida de Sabina, Octavia nos recibía con la ponchera de agua y el lienzo sobre el hombro para quitarnos el polvo y la tierra que traíamos de los conucos. Nosotros nos apresurábamos a rociarnos la cara no fuera a ser que alguna lágrima delatara nuestra debilidad.

A Higinio le dolían las coyunturas. Cada día exponía una razón nueva para permanecer al resguardo del hogar, aletargado y meditabundo; un hombre que pocas semanas atrás se fajaba con el machete, como cualquiera de nosotros. Después, ya no puso pretexto. Se quedaba sentado en su mecedora, en el umbral de la sala, mirando todo el santo día hacia un punto indefinido.

Habían transcurrido tres meses desde la realización de las bodas y la vida de Sabina parecía satisfactoria, a juzgar por las pocas noticias que nos llegaban. Hermógenes había conseguido ocupación en Santo Domingo, ya no tenía que viajar. A diario estaba cerca de su esposa.

Quizá fue una celada de nuestro apego a Sabina el cuajarón de visiones que una noche nos espantara a sus nueve hermanos, pensamos. Sin embargo, palpitaba en nuestra naturaleza otro motivo de incertidumbre: desde ese sueño atroz, no habíamos vuelto a soñar con Sabina. Además, qué le sucedía a nuestro padre. Él no soñaba como nosotros, pero se comportaba como si un mal agüero lo estuviera desangrando. Podía volverse tullido, de tanta modorra.

Hermógenes creyó que la noticia me alegraría: Sabina estaba embarazada. Esto soliviantó el ánimo de los hombres y a mí me produjo sudores fríos y dolor de cabeza, pese a que ardía en deseo por tener un nieto agarrándose a mi falda. Aunque no me habían invitado a su recién establecido hogar, preparé viaje para Santo Domingo. Encontré a mi hija con buena apariencia: el pelo liso y encendidas las mejillas. La pareja se había instalado en una habitación espaciosa —un rincón de la cual se había habilitado como baño—, anexa a la casa materna del hombre y con salida a la calle. Gozaban de lo necesario y hasta de ciertos lujos, como abanico de techo, licuadora y televisión a colores.

(Sabina poseía tobillos como monedas de níquel. Sus brazos evocaban las plumas del pajuil...).

Nuestra atención, por fuerza y destino, se desplazaba hacia nuestro padre, para quien no hubo un momento de sosiego desde la partida de su consentida, del nidal de la casa, de la niña de sus ojos. Con el paso de los días, entre ceja y ceja se le fue clavando la idea de que a Sabina la habían descuajado de nuestro hogar, de que nunca jamás la dejarían acercarse a nosotros. ¿Quiénes han hecho eso?, le preguntaba mamá. Él denegaba con la cabeza en espera de un desenlace que lo rajaría como un rayo a una palma.

Octavia lo mimaba con chenchenes y cajuiles en almíbar. Higinio los probaba solo para no desairarla. Le conseguimos nuevos gallos de pelea. ¿Para qué, si ni siquiera atendía los otros? Por último, cumpliéndose el séptimo mes del embarazo de Sabina, desempolvamos el acordeón y la tambora y nos pusimos a tocar. Nuestro padre nos había enseñado a manejar los instrumentos de música, pero sobre todo a Sabina le había mostrado cómo tratar al acordeón para sacar un ritmo cadencioso. Higinio lagrimeó sin disimulo.

Decidimos armar una fiesta a San Miguel, el patrono de nuestra zona, en gratitud por la extraordinaria cosecha de habichuela que habíamos logrado en nuestra siembra en la montaña y los buenos precios del mercado. Le mandamos un recado al cuñado, para que no dejaran de venir. Por la misma vía nos hizo saber que Sabina presentaba amagos de placenta previa, imposible viajar. Con un nudo en la garganta, les ocultamos la información a Higinio y a Octavia y seguimos con los preparativos de la fiesta.

La tarde del baile, papá instaló su mecedora debajo del mango. No hubo quien lo moviera de ahí. En medio de la algarabía, aturdidos por el ron, la música y las muchachas bonitas, recibimos la noticia. El telegrama lo trajeron desde el cuartel. Venía dirigido a Higinio y solo a él se lo entregaron. A nuestro padre, los dedos le temblaban, voceaba débilmente: "¡Octavia!", "¡Octavia!". Yo, cubierto de un sudor pegajoso y frío, busqué a mamá en la cocina. El mensaje decía: "Sabina de muerte. Salgan para Santo Domingo. Hermógenes". No alcanzamos a verla con vida.

Los hechos habían sucedido rápido. Ese sábado, después del almuerzo, Hermógenes salió hacia Villa Juana a comprar unas herramientas. Sabina se tumbó en la cama a ver una película de Cantinflas, terminada esta, empezó un programa de variedades; ella se quedó dormida. De pronto, la sobresaltó un chirrido tremendo. Soñolienta, abobada por el calor y sorprendida, se dio cuenta de que el ruido provenía del abanico, la televisión y la nevera. Tiró los pies al suelo y se dirigió a desconectarlos. Al primer contacto con los enchufes, una fuerza tremenda la arrojó contra la pared. Al rato, vino la suegra, inquieta porque la nevera se había quemado y había escuchado ruidos en la habitación anexa. Llamó a Sabina. Al no obtener respuesta, pensó que esta había salido con su esposo. Echó un vistazo por la persiana entornada y comprobó que no había nadie en el cuarto. Fue Hermógenes quien más tarde encontró a Sabina al borde de la rústica bañera de cemento. Tenía la carita azulada y los brazos enredados en la cortina plástica, a medio tumbar, como si hubiera estado tratando de incorporarse.

Luego del funeral de Sabina, Hermógenes se preparó para partir a Venezuela. Nunca más quiso pisar la habitación donde se consumó su breve matrimonio y expiró su esposa.

Al sol de hoy, en el altar instalado por Octavia en un extremo de la sala de nuestra casa, nunca faltan una lumbre, céfiro y claveles para Sabina. De cuando en cuando, añadimos hermosos lirios que traemos de la zona más fría de la montaña.

Un día soñamos a prima noche. Veíamos a nuestra hermana con una falda dorada y una blusa crema. El ojo derecho se le había vuelto negro, mientras el otro mantenía el color castaño verdoso. Nos comunicaba que estaba en la calle Sebastián Mará número ciento cincuenta y dos, en Abura. Ignoramos si este lugar de veras existe y dónde podría quedar, pero desde entonces, Higinio va recuperando poco a poco sus bríos y nuestro hogar se llena de atareos y esperanza. No es para menos, hemos vuelto a soñar con Sabina.

ABURA

Translated by Lizabeth Paravisini-Gebert

Hermógenes greeted us and asked if he could please have some water.

I quickly got up to get him a glass, pushing my way past Sabina. A thought flashed through my mind: she'd been waiting for him, even if they'd never laid eyes on each other before. I went to the kitchen, wary. When I came back I was sure they'd established a connection.

"Allow me to leave you a few Coca Colas," he said, finishing his glass of water.

"There's no need," I replied, adding that there was no refrigerator in which to cool them.

Besides, he got what he wanted, my daughter returned his smile.

"When you come back you can bring us some sodas," she said, ignoring my earlier reply.

Sabina was my last pregnancy, my last hatchling. She was born light as a lizard, her sucking reflexes so weak I had to squeeze my breasts and let them drip into her mouth, drop by drop. I couldn't bear to see her completely naked until she was three months old.

***

When Sabina turned five, Higinio, our father, took her to the town of

San Juan to have their photograph taken. He insisted on our mother, Octavia, teaching her to read and write and sharing with her what she knew of numbers. We may have been her siblings, but from the moment we lost our baby teeth, our father beat us to a pulp and forced us into the backbreaking work of planting crops even in the most inhospitable terrain. He made us walk through pitch blackness and terrifying gales. That's how you hone the instinct to dodge a gash from a knife and obtain the grit to work in any situation.

As a child, Sabina spent her time scrambling up trees. Since she weighed so little, she could climb palm trees or swing from mango branches. It's not that she was rough, quite the contrary, her arms were as thin as crab pincers and her eyes glittered like pinecones. She was not without her peculiarities, however.

Many restless children get in the habit of eating dirt, but our only sister would hide under the crawlspace to munch on flowers. Once Octavia, our mother, had to rush her to the hospital because her belly had swollen and she had convulsions. The doctor thought she'd eaten a toxic plant or seed. Wild manioc? Possum wood? Knee holly? Golden trumpet? No one knew what the girl had eaten. The doctor pumped her stomach. To cure her from the vice of eating flowers, our anxious mother mixed a horrible purgative of mashed bindweed and hibiscus and the next day she made her chew rose petals she'd boiled together with *canafistula* flowers, the worst tasting thing we knew. Papá didn't endorse these tactics and made it up to her by secretly giving her candy.

One night, about a month after the incident with the toxic flowers, we dreamt that Sabina was painting the trees in the yard the colors of water while strong winds blew around her. Everything the wind blew, cockroaches or beetles, frogs or scorpions, softened upon hitting the trees and melded into their bark. Octavia and Higinio, from their rocking chairs, watched their pampered daughter's endeavors with complete indolence and pleasure. We, the brothers who dreamt of her in unison, slept at ease in the dream.

Some time later, in anticipation of Mother's Day, not understanding then what the consequences would be, we brought Octavia a beautiful lily plant that grew in the coldest part of the mountains. Each flower had at its center something like a finger covered with yellow solar dust. Sabina managed to eat two of them before fleeing in terror, her tongue sticking out, as if one had rubbed *itchy-itchy* root on it. Her lips and palate were covered in bloody sores and her throat throbbed. She cried for hours. This was truly what finally cured her of the habit of munching on flowers under the house.

When she had her first period, we all dreamt she was wading into a stream. Scarlet clouds were mirrored between her legs. In the dream, it was dusk. In the semidarkness, Sabina splashed water on herself as if trying to get rid of some invisible filth. At dawn we, the brothers, stared at each other in silence while we drank our coffee. In a subsequent dream, three days later, we saw Sabina covered in spots, her skin like a sheet of coconut rice, gliding on a palm frond, her arms open to form a cross and her hair blowing in the breeze. Sawdust spouted out of her. We sighed in relief when the dream ended with our sister gliding gracefully into a pond of crystalline water. Soon after that Sabina came down with measles, which after a week got complicated with pneumonia.

"Don't worry, Mamá. Never mind, Papá. It isn't really necessary to take her to the hospital," we assured our parents. And in fact, our sole sister recovered from both illnesses. By then we had become accustomed to catching glimpses of her at the bottom of our dreams, motionless, most of the time. We watched worriedly; we'd wake up exhausted. Fortunately, it happened rarely. On the very day she turned eighteen, we dreamt of an event that chilled the blood in our veins. At dawn, as we sipped our coffee, we glanced at one another in terror. Our hands and lips trembled. We rushed out to work.

***

Sabina's complexion revealed some lines, as if traced with a bit of indigo. A soft channel springs from the tip of her nose, lightly dimpling her chin and ending at her navel.

***

Hermógenes (his name didn't surprise us), the bottled-soda distributor, came back; of course he came back. Every step, every gesture became a means of marking his honorable intentions towards Sabina. On his third visit he brought our sister a present, which he didn't give her until he obtained Higinio's permission to do so. A few months later he visited our home accompanied by his mother. It was a long visit, during which Hermógenes formalized his proposal of marriage, supported by his mother's exquisite urban amiability. At every point, the woman from Santo Domingo uttered a compliment: "Your kitchen sparkles like gold," she told Octavia. "One breathes such pure air here." "So many fruit trees. One has to be a persistent worker to turn a profit from this land." We held back, silent, not interested in breaching the distance. Higinio smoked his pipe and looked for something to do, proud and intimidated at the same time. At lunchtime, Papá mentioned that some foals had been destroying the corn crop. We all wanted to go with him, to escape, but a look from Octavia (don't you dare go!) sufficed to stop us in our tracks.

Disheartened, we didn't know what to do. And it showed. Sabina, however, looked radiant. Despite our long faces, when we returned from work she greeted us with a smile, with a bowl of fresh water and a linen towel on her shoulder. And while she watched us wash our hands and splash our chests, she brought us up to date on sundry domestic events. Sparkles the color of chestnut stirred in her eyes. We asked ourselves inwardly: why the hell does she have to go with that guy with the truck when she has ten men here who adore her?

We kept our watch, what more could we do? We spied on her conversations with her fiancé, hoping for the man to make some mistake. Higinio lost his peace of mind. He didn't know why, but the instinct of a devoted father spoke to him of something nebulous and strange. The slightest remark would get us reprimanded. Sometimes, when he was having breakfast, his eyes would grow dim with tears.

I asked myself what ill wind had blown Hermógenes our way. What did he know about Sabina? We were the ones who truly knew her. We'd fed her bite by bite and snuggled with her when she'd had a fever as a small child. We'd been there for her in her weakness and had watched her gain in strength, from when it was necessary to hold her little head to keep her upright until her legs grew sturdy and she beat us at races. Each one of us had held her tightly in our arms at bedtime.

"We're going to live very comfortably," Hermógenes would tell us, smiling from ear to ear. And looking at us with his friendly eyes, wanting to say: *I understand, I understand your brotherly apprehensions, but don't worry, I'm going to take care of her and protect her.* Octavia paid him enough attention for the entire family; she listened carefully to every phrase he uttered and to every allusion to their future. Our mother liked the young man and let him know it. That's what she led us to believe for months. She was reserved and knew how to hold her emotions under control.

***

I inquired, seemingly casually, about incidents and cares in Hermógenes' family. He seemed too pale to me, as if he always felt cold. His lips were purplish—I'd heard that's the case with people with heart complaints. But he made no mistakes, behaved with propriety and respect, and I couldn't draw him into any suspicious revelations. His mother was a strong and well-educated woman, we'd confirmed this; his father lived in Venezuela, as did his sisters. The young man had no children outside of marriage, nor had he ever been committed to any hospital. He'd had no trouble with the police. So why did I still feel such a thorn in my heart?

To gain time, I persuaded my daughter that knitting bedspreads, embroidering tablecloths and sewing the clothes she'd wear as a married woman were requirements for good luck in marriage. Hermógenes, somewhat saddened since he'd preferred an early wedding, accepted Higinio's counterproposal to "give us enough time to prepare for the festivities, since the parents of the bride are responsible for the celebration." The fiancé couldn't hide his grief when we raised objections to his taking Sabina to live in the capital. A week before the date set for the wedding, my father died in the countryside near Oviedo, where he'd sought refuge since the times of the dictatorship. I said that Sabina couldn't get married while our home was in mourning. She replied that she'd never in her life seen her grandfather. It wasn't like my daughter to contradict me. There was a new delay.

With the new agreed upon date upon us, there was nothing left to invent to delay the marriage. After all, one cannot twist fate armed only with a dream.

***

Sabina's heat emits winged ants, like a portent of rain. Sabina's heat moves towards whoever feels cold. Her breasts are like guava pulp. Her back seems made of heart of palm.

***

Higinio, taciturn, hid behind his bad mood. Mamá struggled against her emotions, but it didn't stop her from fulfilling her required duties to the letter. She prepared the bath that the bride had to take with zeal. On that day, seven basins of water had been warming in the sun since dawn. Six were filled with spring water, with the following elements added: in the first one there was honey and salt; in the second, bitter lemon; in the third, orange blossoms; in the fourth, camphor; in the fifth, white, red, yellow and pink roses; in the sixth, mint and eucalyptus leaves. The contents of the last basin, in which Sabina was to complete the final rinsing of her body, came from gathering the evening dew in thirty basins during thirty days. The liquid filled only a third of the basin. Octavia herself took charge of the bathing. We followed the operation on the sly, since it was taking place in a room without doors near the main house. We don't know where our mother got the idea that the rigorous bath would protect her daughter once she abandoned the safety of our home. And what if that dream had been deceptive, a sort of trick against Sabina's happiness? Octavia, with her many errands and tasks, didn't leave us any time to think, as if on purpose.

"Everyone should enjoy the party. No one should have a reason to complain about your sister's wedding," she said to us. During the celebration, we took great pains to attend to our guests, especially those who'd come from Santo Domingo to accompany Hermógenes. For brief moments we were seized by waves of anxiety that made sweat run down our faces, seeping into our eyes. Papá wasn't able to overcome his malaise. He moved slowly back and forth like a zombie. The most observant guests were left convinced that he was ill. Not even Octavia could get him out of his taciturn, resigned, and absent state. "It's just that Sabina is his life, and now she's going to be hundreds of kilometers away," Octavia explained to those close to the family.

In the days that followed Sabina's departure, Octavia received us with the washbowl at hand and a towel over her shoulder so we could get rid of the dust and soil we brought down from the land. We hurriedly splashed water on our faces so no tear could betray our weakness.

Higinio's joints were hurting. Lethargic and taciturn, every day he came up with a fresh reason to stay home; a man who just a few weeks before had wielded a machete vigorously, like any of us. After a while, he didn't even bother with an excuse. He'd remain in his rocking chair, on the threshold of the living room, staring all day at a single indeterminate point.

Three months had gone by since the wedding and Sabina's life seemed satisfactory, to judge by the few bits of news that reached us. Hermógenes had found employment in Santo Domingo, so he no longer had to travel. He could be near his wife daily.

The surge of visions that terrified her nine brothers the night after the wedding had been perhaps the result of our love for her, or so we thought. Our very natures quivered with doubt, nonetheless, since after that dreadful dream we'd never again dreamt of Sabina. And what had taken hold of our father? He didn't dream like us, but he was behaving as if a bad portent were sucking his life's blood. Such lugubriousness could cripple a man.

***

Hermógenes thought that the news would please me: Sabina was pregnant. This lifted the spirits of the men but made me break out in cold sweats and headaches, despite my burning desire to have a grandchild hanging onto my skirts. Although they hadn't invited me to the home they'd set up together, I prepared a trip to Santo Domingo. I found my daughter looking well: her hair smooth and her cheeks rosy. The couple had installed themselves in a spacious room—a corner of which had been fitted out as a bath—attached to his mother' house and with a door to the street. They had everything that was necessary and even certain luxuries, like a ceiling fan, a blender, and a color television.

***

Sabina had ankles like nickel coins. Her arms evoked the plumes of the flowering cashew tree...

***

Our attention, by force or fate, displaced itself towards our father, for whom there hadn't been a moment of peace since the departure of his favorite, the home's fledgling, the apple of his eye. As the days went by, he became obsessed with the idea that Sabina had been wrenched from our house, that she'd never again be allowed to be near us.

"Who has done this?," Mamá asked him. He shook his head, as if expecting an event that would rend him in two like a bolt of lightning does to a palm tree.

Octavia spoiled him by preparing his favorite dishes, *chenchén* and cashews in syrup. Higinio picked at the cashews so as not to offend her. We got him new fighting cocks. Why on earth, since he barely took care of the ones he already had? Finally, at the end of Sabina's seventh month of pregnancy, we dusted off the accordion and the *tambora* and began to play. Our father had taught us how to play musical instruments, especially Sabina, who had learned from him exactly how to draw out the accordion's rhythmic cadences. Higinio wept openly.

We decided to organize a party in honor of San Miguel, the patron of our region, in gratitude for that year's extraordinary bean harvest at our farm in the mountains and for the excellent prices we'd gotten at the market. We sent our brother-in-law a message, so they wouldn't miss the event. The same conduit brought us back word that Sabina was showing signs of placenta previa and travel was impossible. With a knot in our throats, we kept the information from Higinio and Octavia and continued with the preparations for the party.

The afternoon of the dance, Papa installed his rocking chair under a mango tree, from where no one could get him to budge. In the middle of the rejoicing, dazed by the rum, the music, the good-looking girls, we got the news. They brought the telegram from the barracks. It was addressed to Higinio and they'd only give it to him. Our father, with trembling fingers, called out weakly: "Octavia! Octavia!"

I, covered in a cold and sticky sweat, went to look for my mother in the kitchen. The message said: "Sabina deadly ill. Leave for Santo Domingo at once. Hermógenes."

We didn't arrive in time to see her alive one last time.

The events had unfolded very quickly. That Saturday, after lunch, Hermógenes had gone out towards Villa Juana to buy some tools. Sabina lay down in bed to see a Cantinflas movie. When it ended, a variety show had followed; she'd fallen asleep. She was startled out of her sleep by an awful squeal. Sleepy, bewildered by the heat and the surprise, she realized that the noise was coming from the fan, the television and the refrigerator. She got up and went to unplug them. At the first contact with the sockets a tremendous force had blown her against the wall. A short while later her mother-in-law had come, concerned because the refrigerator had blown its fuses and she'd heard noises from the other room. She called out to Sabina. When she got no reply, she assumed she'd gone out with her husband. She glimpsed through the half-open jalousie and confirmed that there was no one in the room. It was Hermógenes who later found Sabina by the edge of the rustic cement bathtub. Her small face was bluish and her arms were tangled on the shower curtain, which was half torn down, as if she'd been trying to get up.

After Sabina's funeral, Hermógenes prepared to leave for Venezuela.

He never again wished to enter the room where his brief marriage was consummated and his wife had died.

To this day, the altar that Octavia installed in a corner of our living room never lacks a candle, céfiros and carnations for Sabina. From time to time, we add lilies that we bring from the coolest zone in the mountains.

One day, we had a dream during the earliest stages of sleep. We saw our sister wearing a gold skirt and a cream-coloured blouse. Her right eye had turned black, while the other had kept its greenish chestnut color. She was letting us know that she was living at 152 Sebastián Mará Street in Abura. We have no idea if this place truly exists or where it could be, but since then Higinio has started to slowly recover his energy and our home is filling with activity and hope. Needless to say, we have started dreaming of Sabina again.

Reading the Palimpsest

Chaya Murali

You are a mouse. You have a comfortable home. A dense layer of wood chips undulates and crunches under your paws as you walk. You have shredded some to build up a soft, puffy resting place, where you sleep when tired. When hunger strikes, you can always find something to eat. There is plenty of clean water. Light alternates with dark in a constant, familiar cycle. Your charcoal gray coat shines with health.

Every day, you encounter dozens of well-known scents: the piercing ammonia of your own urine, the bright crispness of fresh wood chips underfoot, the close mustiness of the other mice you live with. All these fragrances layer and intertwine to form an olfactory white noise: the aromatic backdrop of your life. Nothing is amiss.

But one day, something new: your pink whiskered nose twitches as an altogether different smell wafts through the air. It is delicate, sweet. You stop walking to inhale deeply. But the sweet smell quickly dissipates, and before you get moving again, you feel it: a zap, there, in your paw.

That was weird. Kind of hurt, too.

You pad your way over to the water, and lap up some hydration as you wonder what happened. Your roommates look just as bemused as you feel. They must have felt it too. You eat a few pellets of food. You sniff the air rapidly, whiskers twitching. No sweet smells. Just white noise. Hmm. Maybe you imagined the whole thing.

But as soon as the thought passes, there it is again: a disembodied saccharine fragrance. This time you know what might be coming, and right on cue, you feel that painful zap on your paw. Before the day is out, the whole sequence of events happens three more times. The same thing happens again tomorrow. And then the next day. When all is said and done, you have learned something new: whatever that sweet aroma is, it brings the promise of a nasty shock.

Your brain encodes the lesson: We don't like this smell. We must remember this.

*

My email inbox has a custom wallpaper. It is a grainy, old photograph I found in the attic of my maternal grandfather's house. In it, a tall thin pyramid of sepia looms over a large colonnaded rectangular pavilion. An amorphous, massive statue rests within the pavilion, a circle of light glaring off its black curvature. The photo makes for an impractical background. Every time I open a message, the image is obscured. The grayscale washes out the entire screen. It would make sense to swap it out for something more aesthetically pleasing and practical, but I know I won't do this.

I am attached to this photo, to the place it represents. I always have been, with a fervency that I never fully understood. If I ever got a tattoo, this image would be on the short list of possibilities. My most tattooed friend tells me this would be a poor choice: the tower's intricate façade would make for an impossibly messy etching. I suppose she's right. Still, I can't seem to turn away from this image, from this place that enchants me so. The big temple. *Periya Kovil.* Rajarajeswaram.

*

You are a mouse again. Charcoal gray coat, pink nose: to humans, you look almost identical to your father. Your father's life, too, was almost identical to yours. He ate the same food, drank the same water, walked the same wood chips, made a nest with the same materials. His fragrant world was the same mix of piercing ammonia and fresh clean wood and musty bodies. What you don't know is that one day, before your conception, when your existence was barely an idea, your father sniffed something new.

It was pleasant at first, this new, insistently sweet scent. He stopped to take it in. But every time that fragrance came, it brought pain. So he learned that this scent was a harbinger of danger. This scent should be feared.

Of course, you don't know all this. Your father has never told you these stories. And so you go about your life blissfully unaware. One day, your daily roaming is interrupted by a startlingly loud sound. You jump. You squeal indignantly. Your reaction isn't surprising. Who doesn't jump when they hear a loud noise?

What is surprising, though, is how high you jump when that loud noise comes after an unfamiliar smell. You've never encountered this fragrance, have no reason to dislike it, but you find it cloying, saccharine, sickeningly sweet. Unexpectedly, your fur stands on end as soon as it wafts through your nostrils. Another loud noise soon follows. You jump again, this time much higher than before. There is something eerie about this whole thing. You have never known this odor. Yet you can't shake the feeling that this experience isn't new. Somehow, you have felt this before, as if in another life.

*

I was born in a city called Thanjavur. In my mind, it is a quaint town, but in reality, its population is over 100,000. It is a microcosm of India, the ancient alongside the modern alongside the animals alongside the cultural and religious diversity. In the old city, where my relatives live, small open sewers run sluggishly on either side of narrow lanes. Carefully placed flat stones bridge a path to the homes, periodically obscuring the cloudy water and unmentionable offal flowing beneath. One plaza, where the dominant features are a modest temple and the massive ceremonial chariot parked just outside, is overrun by goats. They clamber over the chariot like children on a jungle gym, exercising their instinctual alpine agility in this city on the plains.

On all but one of my trips to India, I have spent time in Thanjavur, where my mother's family settled in the late '70s. 1996, 2000, 2004, 2008, 2012, 2014, 2018. Seven trips. Eight, really, since *Amma* and I

Clockwise from L: The author's mother, maternal grandmother, and maternal uncle

managed another quick visit at the tail-end of our months-long family trip in '96. We were staying in Chennai, in my paternal uncle's home, when she tearfully confessed to me that she missed her own mother desperately and wanted to see her again. Eight years old and bestowed with the simple clarity of childhood, I said, So go see her. We booked a train and traveled southward and inland, to my mother's mother's home. We ate food made by her hand. We braided our hair by the light streaming through the open back door in her black-floored living room. We wore fresh jasmine garlands in our hair every morning and evening. We visited the temples in Thanjavur, including my very favorite, Rajarajeswaram. For a few extra days, I basked in a luxuriously matrilineal world.

On the train ride back to Chennai, my mother gathered me close, kissed the top of my head, and said "*En rajathi*" (my little queen). That stolen trip was the last time I saw my maternal grandmother, who died the next year in a freak accident. She was fifty-four years old.

Thanjavur is not technically our native place, as Indians like to say. The family can trace its roots to surrounding towns and villages: Thiruvaiyaar, Mellatur, Thiruppoonthuruthi. The further into history I reach, the more consonants fill my mouth. Nevertheless, Thanjavur is the only maternal hometown I know. That trip in '96, it became my favorite place, the only city in India where I reliably felt connected to the country. Neighbors recognized my mother, and were delighted to meet her children. Our doting uncles lavished affection, buying us coconut water whenever we wanted and hunting for a palm fruit seller to satisfy my cravings.

In Chennai we sat in our relatives' stuffy flats and waited for our cousins to get home from school, whiling away the hours rereading books and watching cartoons in languages we didn't understand. In Thanjavur we seemed to go on adventures every day, walking to the *aranmanai* (palace), visiting the tailor's shop, browsing for kaleidoscopic art plates and jewel-studded Thanjavur paintings at handicraft emporiums. The summer of '96 had demonstrated that my sister and I, having moved away only four years prior, had become irrevocably American. But being in our mother's hometown—which, technically, was also ours—suspended that fact for a time. Despite remembering nothing of this city where I was born, I felt there what I had naively hoped to feel throughout India: a sense of reunion, a thrill of recognition, a recollection of my previous life.

*

Become a mouse again. This time, you are the grandson of a rodent whose paw was zapped whenever a sweet odor drifted through his cage. You don't know it, but your father was unduly startled by this very same fragrance. It made no sense—why would a mouse be spooked by something he had never experienced, something only his father had cause to fear? But spooked he was. It was as if his father's experience was embedded inside of him. This, of course, flew against the commonly accepted science of inheritance, but your father's leaps were undeniable. Somehow, that zap to your grandfather's paw had traversed a generation.

One day, a sudden clattering noise reaches your ears. Startled, you jump. The sound disappears, and you relax. Soon, though, something you've never experienced: a sickly sweet aroma. Inexplicably, you are immediately on edge. The sound that follows makes you leap much higher than before, frightened of an ineffable something you can't put your finger on.

Once your paws are back on solid ground, you start to think. That fragrance was foreign. You know this. But you also know this contradictory truth: You recognized it immediately. It's as if a memory from another life lives inside you.

*

Rajarajeswaram is a temple complex commissioned by Rajaraja Chola, one of south India's most famous emperors. Dedicated in 1010 A.D., it is an edificial historical register, checkered with art and architecture from empires of the last millennium. It was damaged by Mughal invasions, restored by Hindu emperors, commandeered by Europeans. It is a UNESCO World Heritage Site.

The author with cousins and a maternal aunt at Rajarajeswaram, 2000

I knew none of this as a child. My family has always employed its Tamil name, *Periya Kovil* (big temple). I formed my first conscious memories of *Periya Kovil* that summer of '96, visiting with a three-generation retinue of maternal relatives.

We must have arrived by auto rickshaw, a sort of covered, motorized tricycle that seats three adults uncomfortably and navigates Indian traffic with stunning agility and an impossibly tight turning radius. [We call them autos, the "ah" stretched by a jutting mandible and the "to" swallowed up by the soft palate, destroying any trace of English.] On the dusty external courtyard, a platoon of cycle rickshaws waited hopefully for potential passengers. We crossed over a shallow grassy ravine, the only evidence of the moat that once flowed here, and ducked through a light pink entryway.

The first *gopuram* (gate) grew before us, a wide-based, sand-colored archway covered in sculptures. Divine entities abounded, some many-armed, some in the classical *aramandi* (bent-kneed) stance of Bharatanatyam dancers, some folded nimbly at the waist, arms resting casually on nearby carvings, others with one leg crossed over their bodies and held high with a bent knee, mimicking Nataraja, the god of dance. For five rows the gate rose, narrow metal-grilled windows marching along the center. I could have craned my neck to stare for hours, but I rushed behind my family.

In the next courtyard stood a decorated temple elephant. I scampered toward it with unabashed eight-year-old glee, probably squealing "oh my gosh" in my jarringly American voice. One by one, we held out coins, and the animal plucked them up, curled its trunk into a pachydermine fist, and lightly thumped our bowed heads in a blessing before depositing the coin into the mahout's outstretched palm. To my utter delight, after a brief discussion (and, I realize now, an exchange of money), my father hoisted me onto the elephant's back for a short ride. I must have been wearing the lemon-yellow romper my mother bought especially for the trip, because I remember surprisingly bristly hairs pricking at the bare flesh of my thighs.

Disappointingly plucked off my gray mount, I entered the second *gopuram*, where inscriptions in Grantham, an ancient form of Tamil, bloomed across the stones. I could read neither language: two layers of linguistic disinheritance. Eyeing those inscrutable words, I wondered if my parents could read them, my grandparents, their parents. How many generations had come to this place? Head filled with those who came before me, I emerged onto the vast main courtyard.

Compression. Release. Awe.

Fifty yards ahead rose the largest *vimana*, temple spire, I had ever seen. I stood transfixed by the sheer size, the riot of sculptures, the stately magnificence. In the foreground, a few steps led to an expansive brick-laid dais, elevating the main *vimana* and a columned pavilion that housed a massive black statue of a seated bull. As we filtered past the statue of Nandi, Shiva's vehicle and servant, he gazed toward his master with bovine contentment.

We ascended a wide stone stairway into the temple, and a wash of familiar fragrances tickled my nose: sharply bright floral notes from the flowers in women's hair. Earthy dust in the unlit corners. Sticky residue from hundreds of years' worth of oil lamps. Metallic sharpness from the brass bells. Light sweetness from glistening, freshly cracked coconuts.

Past pillars and paintings hardly visible in the gloom, we proceeded to the sanctum, where a hulking black Shivalingam presided. The deity's Sanskrit name is Brihadeeswar, a portmanteau of *brihat*, meaning vast, and *eswar*, denoting Shiva. His Tamil name is Peruvudaiyar, which translates to "great deity." Still another name is Rajarajeswara, a nod to the emperor. As a child, I ignored these layered names, and saw only the familiar Lord Shiva. A sweaty priest climbed a metal ladder and waved a tiered oil-wicked candelabra before the massive deity, clanging a handheld bell and chanting in a booming, nasal voice. Upon descending, he walked the flames around the group, each of us cupping our palms a safe distance away, then lightly touching our eyes to close the circuit of divinity: Idol. Flame. Human.

Back on the vast courtyard, we began our *pradakshinam*, the ritual circling of the central tower. Walking the temple grounds, I felt instantly at home. I knew I had been to this temple before, as a baby, but this was more than inchoate infantile memories. I felt the first time my parents came here as a married couple. I felt the moment I was born, just a few hundred yards away. I felt the day my father and his family came to my maternal grandparents' home for the *penn paakarthu* (girl seeing) ceremony, to decide whether he should marry her. So much of my generational history was wrapped up in this city, and this city was inextricable from this temple. The rest of India required interpretation. *Periya kovil* felt as natural and familiar as my name.

The last stop was a low-slung, rectangular shrine where frescoes dotted the ceiling. We walked through the shrine to the sanctum, which housed a female idol named Brihadaambal (great goddess), Brihadeeswar's consort. We gathered her blessings, too, and trooped out to the courtyard, where we sat for a few minutes before catching autos back home. I was reluctant to go.

Peirya Kovil, like Thanjavur itself, was the India I had hoped for. The Taj Mahal had been closed for renovations. The relatives had been friendly but distant. But here, at Rajarajeswaram, I felt intrinsically, effortlessly connected to my heritage. I wanted to learn everything about this place, to read every layer of history in the sunbaked stones beneath my feet—my history, my family's history. In this place, I belonged to the country that my parents called home. I felt it had been inside me all along.

*

In 2014, two scientists set out to answer a question: could experiences be passed from parents to offspring? The query seems straightforward enough, but it was part of a scientific controversy that predates Charles Darwin. For over a century, the prevailing wisdom had been that creatures could only inherit intrinsic traits, things like eye color and hair color. Experiences, on the other hand, could not be passed down. You cannot inherit your father's talent for cooking, your mother's interest in Shakespeare.

But by the time Dias and Ressler began their experiments, a curious body of evidence had begun to accumulate. Waterland and Jirtle found that when mice consumed certain dietary supplements pre-pregnancy, their babies' coats were deep brown instead of speckled with yellow. Champagne and Meaney showed that pregnant rat mothers subjected to stress produced offspring who were more anxious than their stress-free peers.

Dias and Ressler wanted to go further. Could a creature's life experiences, before conception, directly influence its offspring's behavior? To find out, they exposed male mice to acetophenone, a floral fragrance. This scent is detected by a solitary olfactory receptor, called M71. They constructed an elegant experiment: if they taught mice to fear the scent of acetophenone, they could look for evidence of this trait in their offspring, not only through behavior, but also through overgrowth of the M71 receptors in their brains.

Fear was conditioned by releasing acetophenone into the cages, then delivering a small shock to the mouse's paw. Then the fearful mice were mated with unexposed females, and their sons were studied. They had never smelled acetophenone, yet when that floral scent preceded a loud noise, they jumped much higher than in response to a loud noise alone. Dissection revealed that they, like their fathers, had thickly cultivated M71 regions in their brains, tendriling outward like generous clumps of saffron. Before being dissected, these sons mated with unexposed females and produced grandsons. Like their fathers and grandfathers before them, these grandsons seemed to fear the fragrance of acetophenone, and their brains exhibited the telltale M71 overgrowth.

In the end, these experiments provided evidence that "ancestral experience before conception" could influence adult behavior. That is to say, we can learn from what our parents experienced before we were even born. We can fear what our mothers learned to fear, love the foods our father learned to love. After all, if negative experiences can be passed down, so too, surely, can positive ones. Our brains are a palimpsest of remembrances, stacked like Russian nesting dolls. Perhaps every moment of *déjà vu* is actually a memory our parents once made. Perhaps we have been here before.

*

Thanjavur is my birthplace because my maternal grandparents lived there. Following regional tradition, my mother came to her mother's home when it was time for her to give birth. The tradition is eminently practical—childbirth is exhausting, early motherhood bewildering. South Indian women come home so their own mothers can help. She bore her into existence. She will bear her into maternity.

And so in her eighth month of pregnancy, my mother boarded a train from Bangalore to Thanjavur, and came home. I conjure her in my mind's eye, thin limbs and full belly, holding my older sister's hand and walking through the train station, riding a sputtering auto across town before crossing her mother's doorstep and finally letting go my sister's hand so that her brothers and parents could envelop her daughter in hugs and kisses. She is achy and tired, but relief floods her, the same relief I feel in my mother's home: She is here. She will take care of me.

Soon, I came squalling into the world after, as my mother proudly

The author's maternal grandparents on their wedding day.

notes, a "totally natural" delivery. There were no analgesics, no new-age birth mixes, no cheerleading family members. Just my mother, the occasional doctor or nurse who reassured her that the pain was normal, and, eventually, me. I was bundled back to my grandparents' home, where my suddenly jealous sister demanded, in no uncertain terms, that I be taken back to the hospital.

On my thirteenth day in this world, my parents named me: Chaya. The name, short and uncomplicated, means shadow. I am told that my father loved the name, landed upon it before I was even born, when my gender was unknown.

As a little girl, I didn't fancy the name "shadow," and preferred the expanded version of my name, unfurling from my tongue like a hidden secret: Chaya Tharangini. The double name sounded trilling, delicate, coy. *Tharangini*s are a collection of Indian classical songs; Chaya Tharangini is an infrequently employed *raaga* (key) in classical Indian music. My unraveled name connected me to my paternal grandmother, a singer, who suggested it.

During the naming ceremony, the father whispers his child's name in her ear. I imagine my slender, teak-skinned, mustachioed father leaning over a small wooden cradle, mustache tickling my ear as he breathed my identity into existence: Chaya Tharangini. What I did not know until many years later was that he also whispered another name: Brihadaambal.

*

In 1809, Jean-Baptiste Lamarck published a book called *Philosophie Zoologique*. He wrote a great many things in the book, but what history remembers most is his theories on inheritance. Lamarck believed that humans and animals could inherit acquired traits from their parents. Think about this for a moment, because it doesn't sound outlandish at first—according to Lamarck, we could inherit our grandmother's arthritic limp, our father's obsession with coin-collecting, our mother's callused hands. Or, as Lamarck's most famous example went, giraffes inherited their long necks from ancestors who stretched to reach high leaves on Serengeti trees.

In Lamarck's imagining, early giraffes had necks no longer than horses'. They roamed African plains searching for vegetation, but they were physically limited to only low-hanging leaves. But one day, a few ancestral giraffes, particularly hungry and particularly persistent, craned their necks to reach higher leaves. Those short-necked ancestors craned and craned until their necks actually elongated. The taller giraffes ate better than the others, leading to a competitive advantage. They were able to reproduce more and, (here's the Lamarckian twist) their offspring were born with long necks. This sequence of events repeated for several hundred generations, transforming giraffes into the species we know today.

When you think about it, this idea is attractive. Wouldn't it be nice if we could emerge into the world with heads full of lessons from our parents' mistakes? In his time, Lamarck's theories were welcomed. People liked the idea that their own striving could improve their children's lives.

But fifty years after *Philosophie Zoologique*, Charles Darwin published *On the Origin of Species*, and his theories quickly superseded the old ideas. Fossil evidence bore out Darwin's proposition. So did DNA. Lamarck became one of the famous laughingstocks of scientific history, a man with fantastic ideas about inheritance, a man who had been wrong. Experience was not heritable.

And yet. Evidence now abounds about the influence that parental experience has on offspring's intrinsic traits. Mice fear the smell that portended a painful shock to their grandfathers' paws. Rats whose mothers neglected them are more anxious in adulthood, and become neglectful mothers themselves. Maybe Lamarck wasn't a flawed scientist after all, but a visionary. He saw something that others didn't see. He saw a giraffe's neck stretching forward in time.

*

The author with her parents, sister, and maternal grandfather at the Houston Hindu temple.

I was seventeen years old when I learned my secret name. My parents and I had come to our local temple in Houston, a semi-open-air structure with pure-white *gopurams* and *vimanas*, tiny compared to Rajarajeswaram. We were inside the central temple building, where my parents had asked the priest to conduct an *archana*, a ceremony invoking blessings for each member of the family. There is a formula to the ritual. The priest chants a few prayers in his sonorous voice, collects fruits and flowers onto a plate, and stands before us. Our fingers graze the edges of the plate, indicating that we are offering its contents to the lord. The priest says "*gothram*?" and looks expectantly at my mother. She provides the name of our family clan. He repeats it, tacking on a few Sanskrit words to declare our lineage to god. Next comes my father's birth star, then his name, my mother's birth star, then her name, my sister's, and mine.

I've experienced the ritual dozens of times. Its predictable script, the familiar cadence of my mother's responses and the priest's intonations, the sense of being formally announced like a member of the peerage entering a royal ball, I find these things soothing. I enjoy listening to my heritage being traced out loud, from the ancient sage who gave his name to our family clan to my parents to my sister to me, all of it in turn reflected back to the divine in a string of identity and inheritance. My mother likes to use the most formal versions of our names for *archana*. Murali becomes Muralidhara Sharma. Swathi becomes Swathishta. Chaya becomes Chaya Tharangini. [Her own name, Lalitha, has no extension.] This titular elongation feels appropriate, like standing up straight to show respect.

On that day, the *archana* followed the usual trajectory, until we got to the space where my name belonged. Instead of Chaya Tharangini, my mother uttered a word I had no memory of: Brihadaambal. The priest repeated this unfamiliar name, then walked back to the idol with the tray of fruits and flowers, chanting prayers with the speed of an auctioneer. Though brimming with curiosity, I had to keep quiet until the ceremony was over.

Afterward, we trooped on through the humble temple complex, visiting two more shrines to complete our circuit. I scurried behind my mother, waiting impatiently as she greeted old friends and inquired after their parents and children, until I had the chance to interrogate her:

What was that name you said earlier?

Oh, that? She replied breezily, in Tamil. *That is your name only.*

I sputtered my protest—*No it isn't, I've never heard that name before.*

Of course you have, she insisted casually. *It's the name of the goddess of* Periya Kovil.

I dimly recalled that the Shiva at *Periya Kovil* had a complex Sanskrit name, Bri-something, but I was certain that my mother had never taught me his consort's name, instead always referring to her as Ambaal, the generic name for a female deity. Oblivious to my confusion, she went on. We gave you that name to remind you where you come from, just like your sister and cousins. All of you have ceremonial names, from temples in Thanjavur, or from ancestors.

I took mental stock: my mother sometimes called my sister Swarna Kamakshi, for the gold-armed goddess of another Thanjavur temple. My cousin Sridhar was also Kamalan, a masculinized version of our grandmother's name. Indeed, most of my relatives were binomial, their daily and ceremonial names markedly distinct. My name only stretched. But now it had transmuted.

The exchange was just like so many others I've had with my mother. I ask a question, she gives an answer that knocks me flat on my back, she's mildly bemused at my surprise, then casually moves on to the next topic while I try to pick myself up. It happened when she reported that her parents are second-degree relatives by blood. It happened when she taught me about the caste system.

I think the intensity of this generational call-and-response is possible only in immigrant families. When you are surrounded by a norm so utterly different from your parents' upbringing, is it any wonder that every cultural lesson feels like a collective secret?

It was only later that I reflected on this secret name's significance. When I had clambered atop that elephant in the outer courtyard, when

I had craned my neck to look inside those grilled windows on the first *gopuram*, when I had stared awestruck at the countless carvings and prayed before the gargantuan deity, when I had visited that low-slung hall and seen a female idol, when I had felt, both inexplicably and undeniably, connected to Rajarajeswaram, of which I had no memory—all along, this place had been inside me, written upon my very existence with my father's whisper. Another entry on the palimpsest. Time compressing to lay past upon present.

*

Rajaraja Chola is standing on a paved courtyard, gazing at a thin pyramidal tower. He is fifty-six years old. He has worn his kingdom's crown for twenty-five years, and in that time he has expanded the Chola Empire masterfully, from Cheralam in the west to Lanka in the south, even annexing Kalinga in the north. His conquests have earned him the name he assumed when he ascended to the throne: Rajaraja – King of Kings. But many years ago, his thirst for military engagements was quenched, and he had turned to religion.

Like his ancestors, Rajaraja is a great devotee of Lord Shiva. He has patronized singers of the old hymns, spreading their glory throughout his kingdom. He has worshipped at Chidambaram, the great Nataraja temple that was favored by his forebears. His devotion is as vast as his territory, and so he decided to build a temple to match it. The temple would be larger than any the world had seen, as glorious as his empire, and it would be located in his beloved capital, Thanjavur.

Thousands of artisans and laborers were employed. The granite was quarried from thirty miles away and dragged to the site by teams of elephants. The *gopurams* and the central *vimana* grew upward, and sculptors covered every visible surface in carvings. Most extolled Shiva, but others reflected the diversity and tolerance of his kingdom: the

images of Buddha, the panels depicting legends of Vishnu. Exquisite frescoes were painted.

As he surveys this complex he has commissioned, Rajaraja feels pleased. He and his family have donated richly to the temple, and Grantham inscriptions bear witness to their generosity. He has set aside money for every necessity, from camphor and cardamom to buffalo, sheep, and cows to provide dairy. He has created whole neighborhoods for the musicians, priests, servants, accountants, treasurers, carpenters, and dancers who will serve the temple, and provided for their salaries. Over four hundred pounds of gold, five hundred pounds of silver, and countless jewels have been provisioned to adorn the idols in great splendor. No detail has been overlooked. No expense has been spared.

On the 257th day of the year 1010, Rajaraja bathes the temple spire with water from the sacred rivers of the Chola Empire. The grand opening. Rajarajeswaram, this monument to his devotion and his empire's greatness, is now a living place.

Rajaraja cannot know what will happen in this place that bears his name. He does not know how the beautiful frescoes will be covered, centuries later, by new artwork commissioned by kings from another dynasty. He does not know that the original Nandi he oversaw will eventually be dwarfed by another, a hulking display of devotion and greatness. He cannot know that invaders with white skin will briefly commandeer his beautiful *gopurams* for a garrison, how Mughals will damage this complex but never succeed in destroying it.

But even as his temple becomes a palimpsest, it remains, a piece out of history, a physical chain linking past to present, a tactile, visual, olfactory memory of where we have been and how far we have come.

A giraffe's neck stretches forward through history. A mouse's life lessons are imprinted on his sons and grandsons. A woman affirms the identity she has always felt inside her. An emperor's legacy lives on.

Go Home

from *Neruda on the Park*

Cleyvis Natera

Months before, Eusebia sat next to an older Dominican woman who talked to the roof of the moving bus they were on, who lamented she had to move to Reading, PA with her cousin because she couldn't afford her rent anymore. At one point, she looked directly at Eusebia. Have you heard of Reading, PA? Eusebia shook her head. What should I do? I don't want to leave my home, the old woman said. Eusebia held the strange woman's hand, silently patting it. That day, she'd been sure it would never happen to her. Why had she thought they were immune?

Today, Eusebia pushed the laundry cart out of her building. It was so heavy she had to use the strength of her entire body as she got it out of the building, through to the sidewalk. The noise from the construction started at exactly 7am, as she crossed the street into Nothar Park. It was deafening. There was hammering and yelling, and huge machines put in place just to amplify all the noise. Maybe it wouldn't be so bad. Maybe this construction wouldn't yield displacement. But what else could they be building but luxury apartments? Fancy, expensive and meant for people who didn't look like any of them.

How would she fix this mess?

At the thought, she felt her body hurled into the air. The cart fell over and she fell to the side of it. Both hands went out instinctively to break her fall, one touched the trunk of the tree on the way down, the other awkwardly slipped on the dirt. A loud thud. Then a stinging pain. Her head had hit the ground. Hard. Then, the weight of the cart, which inexplicably fell over on top of her, all that weight on her head. A gash opened on the back of her head somewhere. Eyes closed, she felt a torrent of blood down her neck, rivulets on her skin soaking her shirt, scarf, and coat. Eyes opened, the blood spread not down like it was supposed to but out, right around her, dispersing into the air. As if the air was made of water. Back when she still had a period, this was the full expression on the third day of her flow: out of her body the brightest of reds spreading in the bowl of the toilet – unstoppable eggs, uselessly escaping her body – a reminder the beginning of life and death often inked the same. This red in the air was just as vibrant, just as gorgeous, the same exact tone infusing the brown of the dry earth, penetrating the root of that offensive tree. Becoming the deepest red she'd seen. The hand that touched the trunk now touched the root; mesmerized, she watched as that hand turned red, then the arm attached to the hand, then her entire body, completely red! Then the park. Then the buildings. Then the sky. How had she never noticed the sky itself was an inverted bowl?

Her friends, the Tongues, appeared above her. All of them tainted red, too.

"Should we call an ambulance?" one of them asked, but their voices sounded far away.

She shook her head. She felt for the cut on her head, felt for the wound, and tentatively, on finding it, put a fingertip inside the wetness. She had to pull away fast, because from the one hand that still touched the root of that tree and the fingertip inside the wound there was no difference in texture. Inside the gash, inside her skull, unmistakably, tree bark.

"She don't look too good," the women said to each other. "We should call an ambulance."

Calm yourself down, she commanded to herself silently. She

blinked hard, to right the world. She tried it again. No change, all still red. Blinked harder still. Stop it, she told herself, feeling the rising panic as the world deepened to the heart of a beetroot. No need to make a big fuss. At the third hard blink, the world went back to normal. Finally, all that red gone. The world back in order. Fingertips went on the side of her head again and felt for – but did not find – a wound. There was not even a cut. Just a tender spot there.

"Let's go to your house," Eusebia said to the women. Her voice thicker, deeper to her own ears. Could they hear the difference?

She stood up and wiped away the dirt from her bruised hand, wiped more dirt from the side of her hip. She offered the women a small smile so they would know she was fine. She touched the side of her head again, the part that pulsed, with cautious fingertips, pressing it to make sure. She was relieved – and confused – when she still found no blood.

She took a step. She stumbled. Two of the women reached for her, then held her by each arm, while the third righted, then pushed the laundry cart, bending to pick and put back all the clothing that fell out. Humiliating, of course. Among the dirty clothes, Luz's undergarments. Now they all knew her daughter didn't wash her underwear by hand.

Halfway through the park, the women noticed a large moving truck parked in front of the building. An English sign on the side of the truck said "Better Move" in red bold letters, and there were lines that made those letters seem as though the truck was already in motion, hightailing it out of Nothar Park faster than a Dominican lotto winner heading back home. The back doors of the truck were open. A few men came out of the front of the truck. One cradled bright blue blankets and several brand new 3-packs of tape. The other pushed a gurney, and went straight to the front of their building, pressing buttons to be let in.

"Luz got fired yesterday?" one of the women said, her tone a question, but also not.

Eusebia didn't respond. Her daughter fired? It made no sense and it made complete sense. Fired over what?

They didn't push. But all three stared at her, waiting.

How did they find out?

She shook her head at them. It could have meant no, she didn't get fired. It could have meant, in the motherly resignation all of them knew so well, that kids ultimately were put on earth to shame, to disappoint. But then Eusebia firmed her mouth to a line. The shake of her head said leave it alone.

It had gotten colder. Without gloves, Eusebia felt the cold accumulate around her nail beds, making her fingertips stiff. The bruise from the fall on her palm became a slight, throbbing pink.

As they crossed the street, a different set of men made their way out of the building with a brilliant white couch, still covered in its plastic sofa cover, a true tell of who was moving out. Veronica Garcia had such a desire to present herself as having upscale taste. Meanwhile, she'd put a plastic cover on her sofa just like they all did.

She'd been wrong that morning, while making breakfast, when she imagined Veronica doing the same thing she'd been doing. While Eusebia prepared breakfast for her family, Veronica had been preparing hers to depart. Eusebia's hip pinched, pulled, made the opposite knee give. Her shirt felt wet with invisible blood.

"Angelica heard the boss tell her it was going to happen yesterday," one of the Tongues said to the white couch.

The Tongues were always right. The only source of news she'd never questioned. But where had Angelica been to overhear? At the new restaurant where she worked? Maybe when everyone left work early to get wine?

But then why had Luz gotten dressed for work that morning? If she'd gotten fired yesterday?

"Veronica's moving," one of the women said, letting her silence win.

"Remember when," another responded.

This was them being kind.

Eusebia remembered when. She wished the women would stop talking for a bit.

The Tongues sucked their teeth.

"Veronica is the queen of the crickets," the women went on to distract, to make light.

It worked because it was true. Veronica, a member of a long tradition of women referred to as crickets in DR. Why would others call them sirens? These women, who would drop their panties for the men – engaged, married – these women didn't care. These women were named crickets because it was their bodies that created so much noise, so much distraction. And just like their insect namesake, with its strong hindlegs, once they caught what they wanted, they consumed, devoured. Years ago, The Tongues saw Veronica put a hand on Eusebia's husband Vladimir's shoulder, and that hand stayed there longer than was necessary. Such a simple gesture, such a clear invitation. It was him, HIM, who took a step away, out of her reach.

"Good riddance, cricket," one of the women said to the couch.

At the entrance of the building, the women were greeted by more cold, as the drilling from across the way grew ever more insistent. The jackhammer cut the concrete foundation beneath the houses. The sound was familiar – a dentist drilling into bone.

The entire building without heat made the dust weigh more, a sting to the eye that forced repeated blinks. To the right, a pile of letter sized manila colored envelopes on top of the useless radiator that hadn't been there moments ago, when they all left the building. One of the women reached for Eusebia's, the first on the pile, and handed it over. From the landlord. The Tongues' envelope was at the very bottom of the pile.

The letter was in Spanish. Had the landlord ever bothered translating a single document for them before? Of course not.

The three women lifted their eyeglass chains and put their readers on.

The building was turning all the apartments into condos. Each resident would be offered a generous buy-out of the lease. Or, sure, they could buy the apartments. Either way, their days as renters were numbered. The noise across the park quieted; they didn't know when the machines had been turned off. Each of the three women turned to Eusebia. The question hung between them delicate as a single string from a spider to the wall.

How to fix this mess?

Inside The Tongues' apartment, it was warmer than the lobby. They didn't take off their coats. They wheeled the cart and left it off to the side, out their door. Their apartment was exactly like Eusebia's, facing out toward the park. The Tongues' home had too much furniture. A couch and a loveseat and a single chair set of imitation French Louis XV tufted velvet in an olive green. There were too many cushions for a person to sit comfortably but Eusebia tried.

One sister rushed to the bathroom and got a wet cloth, wiped away the dirt from Eusebia's forehead. Then tended to her bruised hand. The water was so hot it steamed.

"Can you check the back of my head," Eusebia said, sounding childish to her own ears. "It feels like there's a cut there."

One of the women parted her long hair, searched and found nothing suspicious except a big tender bump. The throbbing on her palm half way up her forearm now, like the spider, climbing.

"We should take you to the hospital just to make sure," the women said, then waited.

All four of them were equally suspicious of doctors.

"I'm fine," Eusebia said.

Relieved, one of the women was already on the way to the kitchen to make coffee. Another turned the television on.

Moments later, coffee in hand, all the women stared at the killer whale with the baby on its back. Right off the coast of the Dominican Republic's Samaná, the orca had been circling for weeks, carrying a dead baby she couldn't let go of. The camera closed in on her, in the background, a scientist's words, dubbed in Spanish. Should we assume all species of whales are tormented by grief?

"What are we going to do?" one of them finally said to the ceiling.

The throbbing in Eusebia's hand had by then taken over her entire arm. She felt a slight numbness spreading to meet that side of her head, where she still felt the trickling of blood. She reached up, touched it, was surprised to find it still dry.

On the television, the whale's baby slipped off her head, and instead of dipping low into the water as she'd been doing whenever that happened, she let the baby go. Instinctively, Eusebia stood up. She placed a hand to her heart.

"She'll go get him," one of the women said. All of them stared at the television as the whale swam on.

They sat in silence for a very long time, the question the women asked pulsing in the air. Eusebia could taste salt in the air, could smell it as if she'd been standing at the foot of that mountain where she'd grown up, where it gave way to a beach. What were they going to do?

Then, as Eusebia stood waiting for the whale to dive into the water, the television's image changed. Breaking news. The image of a young naked boy, no older than Luz's age when they'd first arrived in this country, flashed onto the screen. He'd been shot numerous times, the reporter said, and the alleged assailant carved a message unto his back: Go Home. He was in the hospital, in critical condition. The boy's name, Jose Garcia, flashed on the screen.

Eusebia sat down. She felt light headed. There wasn't much more of this day she could take. On the screen, the whale was back. Where had the calf gone? Where would the current take him? And this young boy, shot so many times? Who would do such a terrible thing?

The three women spoke to each other and to her, but she could no longer listen. From very far away she heard them say 1992 over and over again. They were speaking of a young Dominican man by the same name as this young boy who'd been on the screen. That Jose Garcia had been shot dead by a plainclothes policeman. They were speaking about how violence had taken over the entire city, how Dominicans spilled out in the streets, arms outstretched in anger, closed fists ready to fight.

One of the women left the room, returned with a folder, handed frail newspaper clippings ready to disintegrate in her hands. Metro section of The New York Times. She stared at the words. Some so unfamiliar, others clearly the same as in Spanish with minor syllable differences.

Surprise

Police

Erupts

Calm

"I have to go upstairs," she said.

She picked up her manila envelope, gave the women one last look before she left.

"I'll come back down tomorrow," Eusebia said. "We're going to figure this out. We're going to stop it."

"Stop what," one of them said, eyes on the screen. Viewer discretion was advised before a flash of horrible images of the boy's back came on the screen. Is it a hate crime? the reporter said to the audience, then gave them a phone number to text their answer to. One of the women reached for her phone, responded to the flash survey. Yes.

Eusebia considered the word "home," carved on the boy's back. Who had the nerve to claim a young boy an outsider?

"We're going to stop all of it," Eusebia said. "The building across the street, them trying to sell our apartments. Them trying to push us out of our homes. We're going to find a way to stop it all."

The women looked at her, incredulous.

"What do you mean *we*?" one asked.

"The four of us," Eusebia said, "we're going to stop it."

Upstairs, in her own apartment, she parked the laundry cart in the hallway. She went back to check on Luz, whose door remained locked. She considered grabbing a butter knife, jimmying the lock and confronting her daughter about losing her job. But the throbbing in her head intensified. She decided to leave her daughter alone. Luz was being melodramatic. She had a bachelor's degree from Harvard, a law degree from Columbia University. If there was one thing Eusebia was certain of, it was her daughter's prospects in life. Why did they fire her? Well, it didn't really matter. Her daughter would find another job before the end of the week. Slowly, she made her way to her bedroom, snuck into bed. Had she ever taken a nap during the day in this country? No, of course not. But today, she put her head down on the pillow, and drifted off to the sound of a drill cutting cement, replaying the memory of the entire world stained such a deep red, and asking herself over and over again "How?" How would she stop this mess?

***

Eusebia thought herself the whale. On that king size bed, she squeezed her legs shut – knees bolted, ankles glued – so her feet became a tail. She moved this new tail from side to side slowly, sheet now water, and the lines in the fabric transformed into different shapes as she got pulled further away from her husband, who slept next to her. Her body, in that moment weightless, reminded her of home. Well, Dominican Republic as the place she once considered home. As a kid, she'd sneak down that mountain by herself, ignoring her mother's shouts in the distance.

Who's got eyes on Eusebia? her mother would ask. Nobody, she'd yell back, running as fast as she could.

Through a dark, cavernous dirt tunnel whose mouth lead to a hidden beach, she'd emerge into the light. There were no palm trees on her beach. No white sand. Short bushes with thorn branches crowded the beach – except for a small path. The pointy rocks on the shore, edges sharp enough to shred feet. But they weren't sharp enough for a wild 6-year-old with soles hard as stone. Her body had adapted, too.

She would sprint into the water, body a spear, and dominate whatever got in her way. Eyes closed, arms tight by her ribs. The farther she went, the deeper she swam. Until saltwater became so dense it shoved her small body off the ocean's floor. Then, up to its surface. Nature had a way of winning. But floating, like swimming, was its own kind of release. Its own kind of triumph. Eyes squinting from the salt sting, she'd always come to the same thought looking at that sky: this world is mine.

On the bed, her new tail made a scratchy noise from weakened, dry soles.

Earlier, in the Tongues' apartment, she hadn't allowed herself to think, to feel. Can a whale cry? Can a whale smell her dead?

Eusebia was ashamed she'd avoided looking at the lifeless body as they zoomed in. She'd focused instead on the immense power of his mother. That body behemoth, so black, with only a bean shaped white spot on her belly. Let him go, Eusebia silently commanded each morning that first week, to no avail. Eusebia knew. She knew once that weight was gone, the whale would be able to glide through the water, gain enough strength to jump out in great arcs. Once she let go, she'd be able to indulge her greatest instincts – to hunt. The killer whale is called so not because of its ferocity but because of its wide-ranging appetite. Everything is prey. She stands at the top of the food pyramid. Always the predator.

Eusebia's bed the ocean, she imagined swimming next to that great body, six times her length, thousands of pounds heavier. She moved her tail in an S. Repeated it. Again.

I am with you, she thought. I know this pain of loss, too. For both of them, the hunger, awake.

Nightgown

Sue Rainsford

One day, during this long ago summer when I was twelve, I went looking for my mother to ask if I could go swimming.

It was late afternoon, dwindling into evening, but that baked-earth smell was still rising off the patio stones. It had been another hot, bright day. All the days that summer were just that sliver too hot, that fraction too bright.

There was a little rock pool on the coarse land that surrounded our summer home, and I was in the habit of going down to the coast to swim inside it. I'd slip into the pool and quickly grow slimy, slick. This wasn't the salted water of the sea. Left largely undisturbed by the tide, the rock pool felt like the stomach of a water-beast, and like a water-beast it moved thick and slow.

I was allowed to go swimming on the condition I came back within the hour and didn't swim too close to the pool's farthest side, which was where the rocks broke and the sea came rushing in whenever the wind ran high.

It took me time to find my mother in our big house, and when I did find her I didn't recognise her face.

She was a stranger to me, for a few moments, standing at the top of the stairs. Still wearing her nightgown, that old garment whose silken creases she'd once taken the trouble to press smooth.
Though my mother was a tall woman, and though she stood straight, the nightgown reached all the way to the floor.
I wanted to ask why wasn't she dressed.
I wanted to ask why she was looking out the window.
What could she see?

She'd made eggs that morning and they'd been bottomed-black. She'd laughed, seeing the scorch on them, saying she'd been distracted by some bright coloured thing, by some song-bird singing.
Father's slippery smile all the while showed me bits of burnt stuck to his teeth.
Chewing on the greasy black I'd looked out the patio door to the wall grown thick with roses.
I wanted to be inside the roses.
I knew soft, pink dreams were happening inside their cushion-centred, pillowed hearts.

Do you know about the moon? And about your secret, inside tide?
My mother loved the moon and would talk to me of their kinship, of her endless respect for the big pale planet and its pull.
At night she'd stay out on the balcony, smoking and murmuring.
The things they spoke about—who knew.
Coming in with feet so cold they were sky-blue, little pieces of sky making footfall in the hall.
Tossing her cigarettes like a gaoler might his keys and all the while her nightgown, dragging.

Did you know we all of us have a secret inside tide? You'll feel yours pull on

you, whenever the moon is waning.
This, at least, she was right about.
It drags out particular things, the moon.
Under its magnet rays, certain things come creeping.
Little green caterpillars on a leaf.

Never swim when the moon is full and high.

The tidal pool trapped a good-sized body of water that, depending on the moon and its tug, could be very warm or very cool.
The water was sometimes blue, more often green.
Sometimes seaweed straggled through my hair and I returned to the house a mermaid.
Vengeful and unappeased, as I knew mermaids to be.
Not kindly, fairy tale creatures at all.
Most fairy tales, in fact, have at their heart a lie.

The moon was full but I asked anyway, *Can I go swimming?*
She looked at me and I saw my question land with a twitch in her eyes.
She looked back out the window and the side of her face, mute and still, was maddening to me.
I want to go swimming.
The moon had been bright as the sun, these last few nights, bright enough to guide me.
I'll be back for dinner, but I want to go.
The cloth stirring and shifting around her hips, her waistline.
Mother, did you hear me? I'm going swimming—I'm going.
That long, long nightgown, its lacy hem snagged on a jagged splinter, so that when she jumped, it was pulled taut behind her.
And then it ripped. It ripped, in fact, very easily, the thin tear winnowing right up her backside, the straps come apart so that it fell from her

shoulders.

And so, she was naked when she jumped out the window, and naked when she fell.

The wild thump of my feet on the stairs, running down and down—strange, animal sound.

I had never been allowed to run in the house. I had never heard the noise of it.

Running toward Father because I wanted to have told him already that Mother was gone, wanted to begin this life I understood I'd just now, in these last few moments, been forced into living.

I wanted to go and break the heart of this soft man with his burnt teeth.

And behind me, at the top of the stairs: cream-coloured. Not quite white.

Puddle of cloth.

Pool of moon-coloured light.

Father, the moon has come inside.

Never again would I live in a house that kept its summertime windows open.

No choice but to grow into a woman whose sleep was hot and choked and deep.

A woman who had been a girl who did not pause to grieve her mother.

A woman who would find ways to stop herself from dreaming about standing at that window.

Still.

Before the sound of my voice telling Father.

Before the sound of my feet on the stairs.

Crumpled gown beneath my feet and through its cloth the splinter catching my own bare arch and snagging.

A deep cut that left a trail on the stairs and that would open, unpredictably and wetly, for years.

A wound that did the weeping for a mother who died naked on her belly with the moon all the while rising, making her flash silver, flash red.

Roadside Stop

Christine Tucker

Regina looked down at her husband, Ray, lying half-in, half-out of their car, his face bloodied and swollen, one arm flung up as if he were waving goodbye.

She had picked him up from work in their olive green 1966 Dodge Dart at five pm, after taking the baby in for her six month-old shots. Shots always made babies fussy, so Regina was anxious to get her home and fed and put down for the night. She could hear her whimpering from the car bed on the back seat.

Regina pulled up to the parking lot and waited for Ray to emerge from the maintenance building where he worked on jets bound for 'Nam. He took his sweet time, walking out with his new best buddy, Tony. Regina took this as a bad sign. Those two had a way of egging each other on, a kind of male one-upmanship that wasn't easy to be around. She got out of the driver's seat and into the back next to the baby. It wasn't seemly for a woman to be seen driving two men around.

She and Ray had gone out once with Tony and his wife, Sunja, who was from Korea and spoke very little English. She had heard Tony tell Ray that night that he would prefer a wife who didn't speak at all.

Regina leaned over and put the back of her hand on Carla's warm forehead. Carla looked up at her, kicking her arms and legs, and whined for Regina to pick her up.

"Shush, baby girl. We'll be home soon. That's my sweet girl."

Ray got in and slammed the door, Tony did the same. Neither spoke to her. Ray pulled out of the base, but instead of turning right toward home, he turned left towards the liquor store.

"Ray, honey. I need to get the baby home. She's runnin' a little fever. Can you drop me off?" Regina said.

Ray looked over at Tony. "Did you hear something?"

Tony laughed. "Nah."

They both got out at the liquor store and went inside. Carla was beginning to squirm, Regina knew she was about to start wailing. She picked her up and laid her over her shoulder, saying, "Shhhh. Shhh, little one. Go to sleep now," as she bounced her. She hadn't eaten anything since lunch and she knew the baby would be hungry now, too, and most likely needed a diaper change. She had changed her in the doctor's office, and had exactly one diaper left and no formula. She'd thought they'd be going right home.

Ray and Tony got back in the car with two twelve-packs and that's when Regina knew she was in trouble. They headed out on the highway away from town. Regina looked out the window at the oil rigs in the distance, the tumbleweeds along the side of the road, and the flat caramel-colored fields lying dormant everywhere she looked. The dust that got everywhere, even her eyelashes. Oklahoma was about as different as one could get from her home of Macon, Georgia. She didn't get out much, with the baby and all, but when she did she marveled at how alien it all looked to her. She'd noticed a cluster of men around the porch of the market in town, looking past her like she was a white ghost.

They drove a few miles, Carla getting more and more upset and beginning to cry in earnest now. She tried again.

"Ray. Carla needs a bottle. Please, can we go home?"

Just then Ray spotted a roadside park with picnic tables where motorists would stop and have their lunches when they were on the road. He pulled the car in sharply and told Regina to get out. She did as he said, and began to walk the baby around, cooing, trying to get her to sleep. Her peach-colored rayon blouse was soon wet and sticking to her chest and underarms, her skirt and nylons making that swishy sound they make when you're too hot to be wearing them. The air hadn't cooled at all even though it must be past six by now, and the baby was a little furnace. Sweat beaded up on her temples, and the back of her neck was wet. Regina lifted up her long, dark hair with her free arm and tried to cool herself down.

Ray and Tony commenced playing tiddlywinks with pennies, laughing loudly, chugging their beer when one of them made the penny jump the way they wanted. Whoever lost had to chug a beer as well. Ray looked up from his game at Regina and said. "You look hot, Regina. Take your blouse off. I want Tony to see your tits."

"No, Ray. I'm not taking off my blouse." She turned around and quickly headed back to the car.

"God damn it, I said take off your blouse!" Ray bellowed, stumbling as he tried to get his feet out from under the picnic table. His face was bright red. He had that Irish kind of skin that got red easily and stayed red for a long time. Regina hadn't realized how drunk he was. She slid into the back seat, quickly put the baby into the car bed and shielded it with her body, Carla screaming and thrashing her little body around in protest at being put down.

Ray wrenched open the back seat door and lunged toward her. She leaned forward and grabbed whatever was lying on the floor near her feet and swung it at Ray. It turned out to be the car jack.

Esto no puede ser nomás que una canción

Criseida Santos-Guevara

(A Fragment)

HAY UNA CANCIÓN que traigo en la mente y no puedo olvidar. A veces el tiempo se me va escuchándola y me imagino que yo la compuse. Me pasa con muchas canciones, pero me pasa más con ésta porque así sucede cuando quieres hacer algo para alguien y dices, piensas, esto no puede ser nomás una canción o una carta o un cuadro o un poema o una estatua o un puente muy bonito; quisieras fuera una declaración de amor romántica sin reparar en formas tales. Me pasa cuando la escucho, cuando me siento poeta y quiero escribir, quiero decir más bien, algo profundo, de amor, de amores, de amores, eternamente de amores, y entonces recuerdo, entonces caigo en cuenta que ya existe, que alguien dijo aquello, y cedo, me dejo ganar por las palabras de otros y mejor me pongo a oírlas, a buscar nuevas formas de decir, pero no nuevas formas mías, sino de otros, y eso está muy mal, dicen, está muy mal quedarse esperando a que alguien diga las cosas tal cual necesitas que sean dichas. Por eso lo estoy diciendo, por eso te lo cuento a ti, por eso te digo desde mi ronco pecho, sin resguardo, la historia de mi vida, como dicen los Smiths, "*Call me morbid, call me pale, I've spent six years on your trail, six full years on your trail*", *¿te la sabes?*, *"and if you have five seconds to spare, then I'll tell you the story of my life: sixteen, clumsy and shy.*" Así somos todos, ¿no? ¿O a poco conoces a alguien que recuerde su adolescencia, su paso por la preparatoria o la secundaria como una etapa de gran claridad mental? Con el tiempo más bien te resignas a que así eras tú, así era tu cuerpo, tu carácter, tu pegue o falta de él. Todos los dientillos chuecos, o los pelos parados, o la cabezota en un cuerpo flaco, o la pinche grasita de bebé rollizo que no desaparece.

Muchas veces he pensado, en esas raras ocasiones en que uno suele mirar hacia adentro y trata de picturearse, que no hay persona como yo, así como yo, que hable así, que le gusten las cosas que a mí, que se atreva a hacer las cosas que a mí se me ocurren, que se estrese por la política y por las leyes y por hacer del mundo un lugar mejor, pero que se estrese de verdad, con sufrimiento, no como esos pendejos compañeros míos de la universidad que se preocupaban pero ahorita ya no se acuerdan; los hippies trasnochados fans del Che Guevara y Marcos que pasaban las horas libres levantando firmas para Amnistía y mandando mails a lo baboso para alguna campaña de Greenpeace. Y ahora ya bien bigotones y panzones, y remachadas y restiradas, o con las caderotas, dejan los focos prendidos de su casa "porque pueden", y les vale madres el ahorro del agua y se ponen a lavar el carro con manguera y riegan la banqueta y usan el automotor de moda aunque en aquellos tiempos juraban e hiper juraban que iban a ser agentes de cambio, usuarios fieles del sistema de transporte, *car pool fans* y ene chingaderas más, bien arrinconadas en algún surco recóndito de la memoria; serias intenciones sucumbidas ante el encanto irresistible del poder adquisitivo y la competencia, ésa tan detestable que tenían nuestros padres entonces y nos parecía un defecto de gente adulta necesario erradicar.

Pienso que no, que no hay gente como yo, que hable con toda propiedad y de pronto se sienta incómoda y mejor diga palabrotas y comentarios vulgares, que de pronto adopte otro registro y termine hablando una mezcla entre colonia medio pelo y personaje libresco, con ese lenguaje delator, impostor hasta cierto punto, engañoso, esas palabras tan guangas, tan ajenas a la realidad, tan impropias de una mujer de treinta años como yo, con un amplio repertorio de maldiciones y groserías fuera de su hábitat natural (las groserías, se entiende), porque cualquiera creería que una mujer como yo hablaría como una profesionista promedio sin mucha cultura, con una plática deliciosa sobre trabajos y rutinas, y maquillajes, y brillitos, y los niños, y los maridos, y si quisiéramos pensar en otra circunstancia, pues entonces sería una mujer soltera muy liberada con largas y largas conversaciones obsesivas sobre pitos, fluidos, sudores, insatisfacciones sexuales, la guerra de los sexos y un arsenal mayúsculo de razones por las que sigo soltera entre las cuales resaltaría por obvia el hecho de ser inteligente, ¿no? El drama de muchas fierecillas no domadas, la historia de la princesa encantada harta de besar sapos, presa en una torre, víctima de la bruja "cacle cacle" del cuento cuya única tarea en el mundo es joderse la paz mental de nuestra lechosa, rubia, o morena a la Pocahontas, heroína del cuento. Debería estar hablando como Carrie Bradshaw, o ya mínimo como Mónica Braun: "si no eres dueña de tu cuerpo, de tu sexo y de tu placer estás, en el hoyo," "una mujer necesita un hombre que no se sienta intimidado de una mujer liberada, un hombre con el cual el género femenino se pueda sentir débil," *or some kind of bullshit like this.*

Pero no, no hay nadie como yo, así de violenta, así con todas estas ideas de violencia; los pensamientos de violencia, o más bien las fantasías violentas en las que tomo una pistola, subo a un camión de ruta y encañono al chofer a la vez que le grito, casi a punto de hacerme estallar los pulmones, cosas alusivas a todo este universo maravilloso de "me la pelas, la has de tener chiquita, puto baboso, lámeme el chocho en mis días" y así por el estilo. Y reventarme la vena saltona de la sien nomás del puro gusto de andar haciendo guato, de andarme bronqueando con la gente, ¿cómo la ves?

Pero *it's just me, I'm just obscene*, como si pusieras en una probeta el desencanto, la superioridad lingüística de Morrissey al decir: "*Why do I give valuable time to people who don't care if I live or die?*," y las palabras a la cara, la saliva escupida en el rostro, las metáforas más perversas y no correctas de Eminem: "*You're a fuckin' coke-head, slut, I hate you, I hope you fuckin' die, I hope you get to hell and Satan sticks a needle in your eye, I hate you're fuckin' guts, you fuckin' slut, I hope you die. Di-ii-ii-ii-ii-ii-ie.*" Y la templanza, la convicción de 50 Cent: "*Look baby this is simple, you can't see, you fucking with me, you fucking with the P.I.M.P.*" O las palabras de America Ochoa, A.k.a Ms. Krazie: "no tengo miedo de una puta niña fresa y escuchando tú mis rimas, yo, te rompen la cabeza, yo sí escribo mis canciones, no como una principiante, contéstame cabrona, es lo que quiero, adelante."

Es como si pusieras en una probeta mucha agresividad, y mucho resentimiento, y mucha represión, y pobreza, y muchos estudios, muchos sueños, muchas posibilidades y promesas que nada más no se van a cumplir, ojete que es la vida. Pero así soy yo, la vida no es que no me importe sino que me vale madres.

Pero bueno, *such is life*. Cuando uno piensa: "ahorita sí le estoy atinando, me cae de a madres, a nadie se le había ocurrido esta idea," resulta que en el fondo de una pila de libros estaba el antecedente en miles de páginas escritas en una preocupación simultánea, casi te podría decir originada por los mismos factores. O cuando dices: "te voy a contar una historia," y piensas: "estoy segura que a nadie le había pasado esto," y de pronto navegando en internet te encuentras a otra persona contando en un blog *the same shit*, la misma puta cosa, como diría Mijares: "esta misma historia continúa sólo cambia de escenario." Y entonces sientes que el aire se va, el aliento, las fuerzas. Un golpe en la boca del estómago como patada de caballo te hace comprender que todo está dicho pero pocos nos damos cuenta, y cuando por fin cabe un poco de cordura en nuestras mentes, se nos prende el foco y pensamos: "ah, cabrón, pos sí es cierto, la onda de hoy son los escenarios," y te sientas en frente de un buen camarada en cualquier bar de estos ni caros ni baratos, le pides que no sea culo y te piche una bebida para entrar en calor, agotan la noche con cuarenta mil anécdotas, se pican en la plática, te invita a su casa y aceptas porque no sabes dónde pasarás la noche, en un abuso necesario le vuelves a pedir una bebida para entrar en calor, te apoltronas en un puff y con aire de persona interesante te sueltas contando verdades, porque las mentiras son las verdades, y las verdades a final de cuentas resultan mentiras. O sea, la misma gata nomás que después de una buena revolcada.

Esto no puede ser nomás que una canción

Translated by Amira Plascencia-Vela

(from [1]*Rhyme and Reason* by Criseida Santos-Guevara)[2]

There's a song stuck in my head, and I can't get it out. Every so often, time flies when I listen to it, and I imagine I'm the writer. Well, it happens with a lot of songs. But it happens more with this one. It's like… like when you want to do something for someone and you say, you think, this can't be just a song, or a letter, or a painting, or a statue, or a beautiful bridge, you know what I mean? "Quisieras fuera una declaración de amor romántica sin reparar en formas tales." See? It happens when I listen to it, when I feel like I'm a poet and I want to write, or when I want to say something intense, something about love, "de amores, de amores, eternamente de amores." But then, I remember. I realize it's already been said. And I give up. I let other people's words

---

1 Quoted songs in this chapter: "Yolanda" (1970) by Pablo Milanés; "Half a Person" (1998) by The Smiths; "Without Me" (2002) by Eminem; "Heaven Knows I'm Miserable Now" (1984) by The Smiths; "Puke" (2004) by Eminem; "P.I.M.P" (2003) by 50 Cent; "From the Throne" (2010) by Ms. Krazie; "No hace falta que lo digas," lyrics by Alejandro Lerner, singer Manuel Mijares.

2 Special thanks to Samantha Schnee, Stalina Villarreal, and the 2019 Kenyon Review Summer Writers' Workshops; the Translation Workshop directed by Elizabeth Lowe and Katherine Hedeen made this work possible.

win, and I only listen to them looking for a new voice. Not my own voice, though. And that's not right, they say. It's not right to think someone else will say what you've got to say. So, I'm saying it now. I'm telling you. I've got to get this off my chest. Hands tied. This is the story of my life, as the Smiths say, "Call me morbid, call me pale, I've spent six years on your trail, six long years on your trail." Have you heard that one? "And if you have five seconds to spare, then I'll tell you the story of my life: sixteen, clumsy and shy." We're all the same. Don't you think? Or, do you know anyone who remembers their teenage years, in high school or middle school, as a moment of great clarity? Of course, over time, you give up and accept how you used to be; how your body used to be, how your personality used to be, how your mojo—or your lack of it—used to be. Crooked teeth, or spiky hair, or a huge head on top of a scrawny body, or that damn baby fat that just won't go away.

I've thought many times—in those unusual moments when I look inward and try to see myself—there's no one like me. Just like me. Someone who speaks like me. Someone who likes the same things I do. Someone who dares and does whatever comes to mind. Someone who gets stressed about politics and law, and cares about making the world a better place. Someone who fights—but for real—and suffers, not like my classmates—those assholes from college. They used to care, but they don't anymore. They were the pull-an-all-nighter-hippies; the Che Guevara and Marcos groupies who spent their free time collecting signatures for Amnesty International and sent stupid emails for some Greenpeace campaign. But now they have bushy mustaches, and fat bellies, and perfect nip-and-tuck faces, or huge butts. They leave their lights on "because they can pay," and they don't give a damn about saving water. They wash their fancy cars with hoses and soak the sidewalks, too. Of course, in the past they swore—with pinky fingers—they'd change the world. They'd faithfully use public transportation and carpool—so much bullshit buried in a forgotten corner of their memories. Their good intentions banished the moment they gave in to the irresistible capitalistic charms of buying and competition, those despicable traits our parents showed us back then, and we thought they were older people's faults we had to fight and get rid of.

No, I don't think there's someone like me. Someone who speaks properly at first, but suddenly feels uncomfortable and starts swearing and making rude remarks. Someone who suddenly adopts another register and speaks a fusion of hood slang and the voice of a character in a book. Someone with that snarky, deceiving, even fake, language. Those rambling words, so far from reality, so inappropriate for a thirty-year-old woman like me, with a broad repertoire of curses and profanities that seem out of their natural habitat (the profanities, obviously). Because everybody would think that a woman like me would speak like an average professional woman portraying a delightful conversation about jobs, and routines, and makeup, and glitter, and children, and husbands. Or if we'd like to think about me in a different way, then I'd be a liberal single woman having quite long, obsessive conversations about cocks, fluids, sweats, sexual dissatisfactions, war of the sexes, and an arsenal of reasons to justify why I'm still single; the fact of being intelligent would be the most obvious one, right? The drama of many untamed beasts; the story of the enchanted princess—sick of kissing toads— locked up inside a tower, victim of the witch (cackle, cackle) whose only task in this world is to screw with the mental peace of the milky blonde—or brunette, in a Pocahontas style—heroine of our tale. I should be talking like Carrie Bradshaw, or at least like Monica Braun, "if you don't own your body, your sex, and your pleasure, you're fucked up." Or "a woman needs a man that does not feel intimidated by a liberated woman, a man with whom the female gender may feel weak." Or some pendejada.

But no, there isn't anyone like me; as violent as me, with all these ideas of violence, thoughts of violence, or rather violent fantasies, such as that one where I take a gun, get on a bus, and point the gun at the bus driver and I shout—making my lungs blow up—all kind of things related to this wonderful sexual universe, "Go fuck your mother! You must have a tiny dick, huh? Goddamn fag! Suck my pussy while I'm on the rag." Or something similar. I'd be shouting to the point of making my veins pop out my temple just because I like to mess around, see?

"But it's just me, I'm just obscene." My personality is like a test tube that mixes inside it a great deal of disappointment with Morrissey's superior linguistic talents, "Why do I give valuable time to people who don't care if I live or die?" Or with Eminem's words spit on your face —with his most depraved and inappropriate metaphors— "You're a fuckin' cock-head slut, I hope you fuckin' die, I hope you get to hell and Satan sticks a needle in your eye, I hate your fuckin' guts you fuckin' slut, I hope you die. Die." Or with 50 Cent's coolness and conviction, "Look baby this is simple, you can't see, you fucking with me, you fucking with a P.I.M.P." Or with America Ochoa's words (A.K.A. Ms. Krazie), "no tengo miedo de una puta niña fresa y escuchando tú mis rimas, yo, te rompen la cabeza, yo sí escribo mis canciones, no como una principiante, contéstame cabrona, es lo que quiero, adelante."

Again, think in a test tube and mix inside it a great deal of aggressiveness and resentment, a lot of repressions, poverty, education, and plenty of dreams and promises that would not come through. Life's a bitch. But that's me. It's not "I don't care about life", but "me vale madres."

Anyway, such is life. Just when one thinks, "I'm on a roll. I get it now. I've got my shit together. Nobody has done this before," there's evidence proving it's been done already. Thousands of written pages and forgotten book stacks attest to it, tracing back resembling worries, and I could tell they have the same origin. Or, what about when you say, "I'm going to tell you a story," and you think, "I know nobody's been there, done that." But then, while surfing the Internet, you find someone else's blog describing the same shit, la misma puta cosa, as Mijares would sing, "esta misma historia continua, sólo cambia de escenario." That's the moment when you feel short of breath, gasping, with no strength to keep on fighting. A punch in the stomach makes you see that everything's been said, although not everybody grasps it. But even after this realization hits you, there comes an enlightening moment, and that's when you think, all of a sudden, "Heck, wait! Not all is lost. What's important today is to be seen, to be on stage, to perform." So, you get to a bar (not too cheap, not too expensive), sit down with an old friend, and ask him to get you a beer (to warm you up). There you are, excited and filling the hours talking; a thousand stories come back and forth between you two over the late hours, until he asks you to go home with him, and you accept because you don't know where you're spending the night. Taking some advantage, you ask him to get you a new drink (to warm you up). You get comfortable and plop down in a puff feeling all V.I.P., and you start blabbing your unvarnished truth. Because truths become lies and lies become truths, in the end, all is the same. Es la misma gata revolcada.

Contributors

Lorraine Avila is an Afro-Kiskeyana born and raised in the Bronx. A literacy educator. A lifelong storyteller. Lorraine graduated from Fordham University with a degree in English and Middle East studies and a minor in Creative Writing. In 2017, she received her Master's degree from New York University in teaching. In 2019, she became one of The Wing Scholarship Program's recipients. Her writing has been published in *Hippocampus Magazine*, *Moko Magazine*, *The GirlMob*, *La Galeria Magazine*, and *Blavity*. Lorraine currently resides in the Bronx, New York.

Yvette Benavides is a professor of English and creative writing at Our Lady of the Lake University in San Antonio, Texas. She is a book critic for the *San Antonio Express News* and a contributor on Texas Public Radio.

Rosa Boshier is a multi-genre writer. Her work can be found in *Entropy*, *The Acentos Review*, *The Rattling Wall*, *Necessary Fiction*, *Ghost Parachute*, and *New Delta Review*, and is forthcoming in *The Los Angeles Review of Books*. Her plays have been staged at The Getty Center in LA and The Mission Cultural Center for Latino Art in San Francisco. She earned her MFA in Creative Writing at The California Institute of the Arts, where she teaches Latinx Studies. She has received support/

artist residencies from the Rainin Foundation, Zellerbach Foundation, Bill Graham Foundation, Maker City LA, and Hannacc in Barcelona, Spain.

Myriam Gurba lives in California and loves it. She teaches high school, writes, and makes "art." NBC described her short story collection *Painting Their Portraits in Winter* as "edgy, thought-provoking, and funny." She has written for *Time*, KCET, and *The Rumpus*. Wildflowers, compliments, and cash make her happy.

Ángela Hernández Nuñez was born in Buena Vista, Jarabacoa, in May 1954. A chemical engineer with a degree from the Universidad Autónoma de Santo Domingo, she found her true vocation in literature. She is a poet, short story writer and novelist, and has written numerous essays on women and literature. She is also passionate about cinema and photography. She has won several awards and is a member of the Dominican Academy of Language.

Yalitza Ferreras is a recent Steinbeck Fellow in Creative Writing at San Jose State University. Her writing appears in *Best American Short Stories 2016*, *Colorado Review*, and the anthologies *Wise Latinas: Writers on Higher Education* and *Daring to Write: Contemporary Narratives by Dominican Women*. She received an MFA in Creative Writing from the University of Michigan where she won the Thesis Prize, and is the recipient of fellowships and awards from Yaddo, Djerassi Resident Artists, Blue Mountain Center, Barbara Deming Memorial Fund for Women, San Francisco Writers' Grotto, and Voices of Our Nation.

Chaya Murali is a pediatric geneticist and personal essayist living in Houston. Her work has appeared in *Crack the Spine* and *Entropy*, and her essay "Bits and Pieces" was nominated for a Pushcart Prize in 2012. She attended the Bread Loaf Writers' Conference in 2018. Chaya writes about identity, inheritance, family, and genetics. She loves cooking, hates cilantro, and can be found musing on food and culture at instagram.com/akkashouse.

Cleyvis Natera was born in the Dominican Republic and grew up in Harlem, NYC. She's the mother of two resilient kids and wife to a smart and handsome guy. She's an endurance athlete who believes fitness is critical to achieving true equality for women. She has an MFA from NYU in fiction and has received writing fellowships/scholarships from The Juniper Institute at UMass Amherst, Virginia Center for the Creative Arts (in VA and France), and VONA (Voices of Our Nation Arts Foundation). She is equally split in her passion for books, coffee and wine. Cleyvis recently completed her first novel, *Neruda on the Park*, and is in search for its home.

Wura-Natasha Ogunji (Cover Artist) is a visual artist and performer. Her works include drawings, videos and public performances. Her work is deeply inspired by the daily interactions and frequencies that occur in the city of Lagos, Nigeria, from the epic to the intimate. Ogunji's performances explore the presence of women in public space; these often include investigations of labor, leisure, freedom and frivolity. She is an Artist-Curator for 33rd Sao Paulo Bienal and most recently performed at Cape Town Art Fair. Selected exhibitions include: Lagos Biennial; Kochi-Muziris Biennale; 1:54, London & New York; Seattle Art Museum; Brooklyn Art Museum; and Louisiana Museum of Modern Art, Denmark. Ogunji is a recipient of the prestigious Guggenheim Foundation Fellowship and has received grants from The Pollock-Krasner Foundation; The Dallas Museum of Art; and the Idea Fund. She has a BA from Stanford University [1992, Anthropology] and an MFA from San Jose State University [1998, Photography].

Lizabeth Paravisini-Gebert works in the fields of literature, ecocriticism and environmental history, art history, and cultural studies. She specializes in the multidisciplinary study of the Caribbean. She is based in the Hispanic Studies Department at Vassar College. She is currently working on a new book project: *The Amazon Parrots of the Caribbean: An Environmental Biography* and on a translation of Dominican author Pedro Vergés' 1982 novel, *Solo cenizas hallarás* with her friend and colleague Margarite Fernández Olmos.

Amira Plascencia-Vela is an independent translator and researcher. She has taught Spanish Language and Translation at college level in the United States, Canada, and Mexico. She has translated Children's Books from English into Spanish; *Rhyme & Reason* is her first attempt to translate a literary work from Spanish into English. She has a Ph.D. in Hispanic Studies from the University of Houston.

Sue Rainsford's debut novel, *Follow Me To Ground*, which received the Kate O'Brien Award and is long-listed for the Desmond Elliot and Republic of Consciousness Awards, is available from New Island Books, and is forthcoming in the UK with Doubleday and the US with Scribner. She was awarded the Macdowell Colony Fellowship (2019). She is writer-in-residence at Roscommon Arts Centre (2018-19), and was recently appointed writer-in-residence at Maynooth University for 2019-2020.

Criseida Santos-Guevara is a México-U.S border writer. She received Honorable Mention in the Binational Young Novel Frontera de Palabras / Border of Words Award in 2008 with *Rhyme & Reason* (Conaculta 2008). Also, she is the winner of the 2013 Literal Novel Prize with *La reinita pop no ha muerto / The Little Queen of Pop is not Dead* (Conaculta

/ Literal Publishing 2013).She holds an MFA in Creative Writing from the University of Texas at El Paso. She is currently studying Hispanic Studies with an emphasis on creative writing at the University of Houston.

Christine McDowell Tucker is a writer, painter, and retired clinical psychologist from Charlottesville, Va. She is the author of a short story collection entitled *The End*, and is finishing her debut novel, *Family Systems.*

Acknowledgments

"Pastelitos" will appear in *Malcriada & Other Stories*

"Go Home" will appear in *Neruda on the Park*

"Abura" first appeared in *How to Gather the Shadows of the Flowers: Short Stories*

"Esto no puede ser nomás que una canción" first appeared in *Rhyme & Reason*

www.ingramcontent.com/pod-product-compliance
Lightning Source LLC
Chambersburg PA
CBHW030643190726
48286CB00008B/2636

* 9 7 8 1 9 4 2 5 4 7 1 1 2 *